# CRIMINAL WOMEN

| | | |
|---|---|---|
| Barking | 8724 8725 | Thames View 8270 4164 |
| Fanshawe | 8270 4244 | Valence 8270 6864 |
| Marks Gate | 8270 4165 | Wantz 8270 4169 |
| Markyate | 8270 4137 | Robert Jeyes 8270 4305 |
| Rectory | 8270 6233 | Castle Green 8270 4166 |
| Rush Green | 8270 4304 | |

-9 JUN 2010

1 1 JAN 2011

2 1 FEB 2011

3 1 MAR 2012

-6 JUN 2013

2 8 JUL 2015

1 1 FEB 2016

# CRIMINAL WOMEN

*Famous London Cases*

## JOHN J EDDLESTON

First published in Great Britain in 2010 by
Wharncliffe Books
an imprint of
Pen & Sword Books Ltd
47 Church Street
Barnsley
South Yorkshire
S70 2AS

Copyright © John J Eddleston 2010

ISBN 978 1 84563 111 6

Typeset in the UK by
Mac Style, Beverley, East Yorkshire

Printed and bound in the UK by
CPI

Pen & Sword Books Ltd incorporates the Imprints of Pen & Sword
Aviation, Pen & Sword Maritime, Pen & Sword Military,
Wharncliffe Local History, Pen and Sword Select, Pen and Sword
Military Classics and Leo Cooper.

For a complete list of Pen & Sword titles please contact
PEN & SWORD BOOKS LIMITED
47 Church Street, Barnsley, South Yorkshire, S70 2AS, England
E-mail: enquiries@pen-and-sword.co.uk
Website: www.pen-and-sword.co.uk

# Contents

# Acknowledgements

I would like to thank a number of people who assisted me in the preparation of this volume.

First, I would like to thank my wife, Yvonne, who proof read every story, suggested improvements, and ensured that I worked to a deadline.

I would also like to thank the staff at The National Archives at Kew, who seem to do all they can to help researchers. It is always a pleasure to visit, and one is always made welcome.

Finally, I would like to thank my publishers, Pen and Sword Books Limited, especially Rupert Harding, and also Brian Elliott, who prepared the final proofs.

# Introduction

**I**s it a truism that men and women have always been equal under the law? Whilst it may well be true that in this present day and age the sexes are treated with equality in British courts, it can be argued that this was not always the case. This is due to a number of factors, which include: the judicial procedure; how women were perceived by society; the types of crime they committed; and the punishments available. Let us consider each of these in turn.

**The perception of women in society.**
For hundreds of years, men and women were thought to have fundamentally different emotional make-ups, qualities and virtues. Thus, men were the stronger sex, and consequently were perceived to be more intelligent and possess greater courage. Women were more governed by their emotions and were, therefore, modest, chaste and compassionate.

This type of belief led to different social expectations of behaviour. Men were expected to be more violent, and self-centred, and thus more easily prone to commit criminal acts. Women were not expected to exhibit this type of behaviour and consequently, when they did fall foul of the law, they were believed to have succumbed to their emotional side.

The roles of the sexes were looked upon as completely different. Men were the providers who brought money into the house and protected their families. Women were responsible for the upbringing of the children. It is true that many women were forced to seek work, but the opportunities available to them were much reduced. They were domestic servants, teachers, nurses and worked in such trades as clothing manufacture and repair.

## Crime and Gender

Men, it seems, were expected to be capable of any crime, including murder, rape, burglary, highway robbery, theft and a dozen other such felonies. They tended to be more mobile within society, whereas women were believed to be tied to the home. This, in turn, suggested that the types of crime that women might commit were based around the home, or possibly their locale. Thus, they were charged with such offences as pickpocketing, receiving stolen goods, prostitution, keeping brothels, concealing births and performing abortions. In practice, with the exception of certain offences such as rape, women and men committed the same sort of crimes, though arguably in different numbers.

## Punishment

Most readers will be aware that until the mid-1960s, certain offences could be punished by judicial hanging. Capital punishment had long been a feature of British justice, and both men and women suffered death at the end of a rope in the twentieth century. Before this, however, certain other punishments would be available to the judge, depending on the offence committed. As to how the law treated the sexes differently, perhaps some basic statistics will illustrate this point.

Research in the Old Bailey records, from 1700 to 1900, reveals details of 114, 292 criminals who were found guilty of various offences. The basic table below shows how these individuals were divided by sex.

At first glance, it would seem that far less women were found guilty of crimes, but it must be remembered that this does not

|  | *Number* | *Percentage of Total* |
| --- | --- | --- |
| Men | 100944 | 88.32 |
| Women | 13348 | 11.68 |
| Totals | 114292 | 100.00 |

mean that women committed substantially less crime than men. The figures do not include those who were found not guilty, and it may well be that juries were more sympathetic towards women. Though it is undoubtedly true that men did break the law more, there was also more reluctance to prosecute women. However, once women did face prosecution, their treatment was not substantially different to that of the men. Perhaps this can best be illustrated by a more detailed examination of these figures in relation to the punishments received in relation to each sex.

## Men

|                      | *Number* | *Percentage*       |
| -------------------- | -------- | ------------------ |
| Guilty               | 100944   |                    |
| Death                | 6116     | 6.06               |
| Executed             | 3391     | 55.44 (Of these)   |
| Prison               | 50064    | 49.60              |
| Transported          | 29328    | 29.05              |
| Corporal Punishment  | 6272     | 6.21               |
| Miscellaneous        | 6677     | 6.61               |
| None                 | 2486     | 2.46               |
| Unknown              | 1        |                    |

## Women

|                      | *Number* | *Percentage*       |
| -------------------- | -------- | ------------------ |
| Guilty               | 13348    |                    |
| Death                | 1015     | 7.60               |
| Executed             | 249      | 24.53 (Of these)   |
| Prison               | 7313     | 54.79              |
| Transported          | 3160     | 23.67              |
| Corporal Punishment  | 541      | 4.05               |
| Miscellaneous        | 943      | 7.06               |
| None                 | 376      | 2.82               |
| Unknown              | 0        |                    |

By comparing these two tables it will be seen that there are, perhaps, just two significant figures. Once found guilty, women were actually more likely to be sent to prison and, once sentenced to death, were also much more likely to be reprieved. Of course, one of those statistics is dependent upon the other since, once a death sentence had been respited, a sentence of imprisonment would be substituted. This would seem to indicate that, to a large extent, the law did treat both sexes equally, but other factors must also be borne in mind.

The first of these factors relates to the death sentence itself, for certain offences. A man or a woman found guilty of, say, the murder of a shopkeeper, would be subject to the same sentence of death by hanging. This did not apply, though, to certain types of murder.

If a man were to murder his wife, then he would still be charged with the simple act of murder and face the hangman's noose. For a woman to kill her husband, however, was a different matter. Since women were looked upon as a kind of possession of their husbands, then they would be charged with a form of treason, known as *Petit Treason*, and the sentence for that was to be burnt at the stake. It is true that almost always, the poor miscreant was first strangled, by a merciful executioner, before the flames could reach her, but there were cases where this practice failed and the woman was actually burned alive. Indeed, such a case lies within the pages of this book.

As a further example, consider the types of murder usually committed. Whilst it is true that there were women who killed for gain, during robberies, for revenge etc., there were many more cases where circumstances led them to commit the crimes they did. Thus, there were many cases of unmarried mothers at their wits end, killing their new-born babies, or of female abortionists trying to assist pregnant women and killing the mother, along with the unborn child. There were also those who would dispose of children, for a fee. Whilst many of these 'baby farmers' were kind and considerate to the children who came into their care, others would simply kill the children as the easy way out. Many may think this practice died out in the early days of Victoria's reign, but within these pages, I detail a case of baby farming from as late as 1903.

This book runs, in effect, from the year 1700, to the last execution of a woman in this country, that of Ruth Ellis, in 1955. One final table may illustrate for the reader just how women fared before the law in less enlightened times.

I am aware of fifty-five women who were charged with various offences and appeared at the Old Bailey in the first of those years: 1700. Here is what happened to those faceless defendants.

What offences were these unfortunate women accused? This may illustrate how women really fared within society itself. Two offences are actually not known, since the records are lost, leaving us with fifty-three women who stood in the dock. Of these fifty-three, one was charged with murder, one with bigamy, one with highway robbery, two with coining, and five with burglary. The remaining forty-three were all charged with theft. Could it be that the way society treated women led to so many falling foul of the law out of pure necessity? In short, were they forced to steal in order to survive, and so those were largely the offences which caused them to be taken to court.

Of the eight death sentences handed down, one was for murder, two were for coining and five were for theft. The two death sentences actually carried out were those of Elizabeth

|  | Number | Percentage |
| --- | --- | --- |
| Accused | 55 | |
| Guilty | 25 | 45.46 |
| Not Guilty | 30 | 54.54 |
| | | |
| *Of the 25 Guilty* | | |
| Death/Respited | 6 | 24.00 |
| Executed | 2 | 8.00 |
| Branded | 9 | 36.00 |
| Whipped | 8 | 32.00 |
| | | |
| Total | 25 | 100.00 |

Green who was hanged on 31 January, for theft, and Catherine Truerniet, who was hanged for murder on 19 July.

Women may have committed less violent crime, but they were certainly a match for the men when it came to theft, burglary, forgery, coining and the like. It might be argued that the only difference was that the authorities relied heavily on the belief, that women were more emotional and so entitled to a somewhat more merciful viewpoint.

The twenty-five chapters of this book cover the stories of twenty-nine women. The crimes they were charged with range from murder, through to forgery and riot; and to fraud and theft. At least ten were executed for crimes that, in some cases, would not even end in a prison sentence today. Their stories may illustrate how women were treated by the law, but equally they may document the more enlightened attitude that the same law demonstrates today.

CHAPTER 1

# Catherine Hayes
## 1726

Catherine Hayes was born near Birmingham in the year 1690. By the time she had become a teenager, Catherine already showed signs of being a voluptuous and attractive girl, and soon discovered that she was popular with men. In due course she ran away from home and settled in Great Ombersley in Worcestershire. Now fifteen years of age, Catherine earned her living as a prostitute, being well known in the nearby army camp.

It appeared that Catherine alternated her life between periods of prostitution and domestic service, and soon she had moved on again, becoming a servant to a farmer named Hayes, who lived some four miles from Worcester city.

The Hayes family were very well off and Catherine decided to use her charms on the younger of Mr Hayes' two sons. John Hayes was captivated by the young attractive woman, and they soon agreed to marry. Fearful that his parents would not approve, John married Catherine in secret.

For a time, they seemed happy enough but soon it became clear that this comfortable life wasn't enough for Catherine. Some six months after they had married, she insisted that they should abandon the rural farm life and move to London. John was duly persuaded and, in 1719, set himself up as a coal-merchant, pawnbroker and money-lender, in Marylebone.

The business thrived and Catherine led a most comfortable life but this, it seems, was still not enough for her. She demanded more money and servants, but John Hayes would have none of it. Indeed, so angry did he become by her constant demands that he actually reduced her allowances. This only served to lead to fresh arguments. Still, Catherine did have at least one thing to console her. In 1725, she had persuaded John to take in a lodger, eighteen-year-old Thomas Billings. Unbeknown to John, Thomas was Catherine's illegitimate son. Furthermore, Catherine now embarked on an incestuous relationship with Billings.

After some time, Catherine persuaded John to allow another lodger to stay with them. This man, named Thomas Wood, was a close friend of Billings. In time, however, he also grew to be rather close to Catherine and soon he too was having an affair with his landlord's wife. Even this was not enough for Catherine who now decided that she would be better off without her husband altogether. Of course, she could simply have left him and gone to live elsewhere, with one, or both of her lovers, but Catherine decided that he had to die. At least that way she would inherit all his property. Over a number of weeks she mooted the idea to her two lovers and eventually they agreed to help.

The plan was put into action on 1 March 1726. Billings and Wood took John Hayes out drinking and, by means of betting who could drink the most, soon had him completely under the influence of alcohol. A semi-conscious John was taken home by his two lodgers and placed gently into his bed. Then, just as he was drifting off to sleep, Billings took an axe and struck John on the head.

The blow did not kill John Hayes, who immediately screamed out very loudly. Another blow from the axe was delivered and this finally finished John off. The question now was how to dispose of the body.

Wood was a butcher by trade so he found it a simple task to cut the body into pieces. The various body parts were then dumped into a pond at Marylebone, but the head, the one part which might cause the body to be identified, was thrown into the River Thames, at Millbank. Unfortunately for the killers, the head came to rest on a sandbank, in Westminster, from where it was recovered by the authorities.

In these days before photography, how could the head be identified? The authorities decided that the best way was to place it on public exhibition. So, the battered head was placed on a spike in St Margaret's churchyard. There it was seen each day by hundreds of passers-by, and eventually no fewer than three witnesses came forward to say that they believed the head to be that of John Hayes.

As a matter of course, Catherine Hayes was now questioned and she told officers that her husband was away on business. However, one of the men who had recognised the head, a Mr Ashby, had had a business appointment with John, who he said would not simply have gone away without telling him. Once again, the authorities visited Catherine's house where they found her in bed with Thomas Billings. They were both arrested and, a few days later, Wood too was taken into custody.

On 16 April, an inquest into John Hayes' death concluded that he had been a victim of wilful murder and his wife, Billings and Wood were named as those responsible. Catherine and Billings maintained that they were completely innocent of any involvement in John's death, but Wood told a completely different story.

Wood readily admitted his part in the crime and said that it had been Catherine who gave him and Billings the money to get John drunk. He also claimed that it had been Billings who struck the fatal blows but admitted that it had been he, as a butcher, who had cut the body into pieces. Catherine, apparently, had been kind enough to hold a candle so that he had enough light whilst he performed the terrible deed. Faced with this testimony, Catherine then also admitted her guilt, but claimed that the Devil had made her do it.

All three defendants faced their trial at the Old Bailey, in April. Billings and Wood were both charged with murder, but Catherine was charged with the more serious crime of petty treason. She claimed, in her defence, that she had not taken part in any of the actual murder itself, but admitted suggesting that John should be done away with, and to holding the candle whilst his body was dismembered.

Catherine also claimed that the reason she had suggested that John Hayes should be killed was partly due to the way he had treated her. He had prevented her from reading her Bible and had only ever allowed her to go to church on two or three occasions all the time they had been together. He had also offered her violence and once, when she had been pregnant, his treatment of her had caused her to lose the child.

Despite these protestations, the jury had little difficulty in adjudging all three to be guilty. Wood and Billings were sentenced to be hanged, and their bodies afterwards gibbeted. Catherine was sentenced to be burned alive, the standard punishment for treason. In fact, Wood never did face the ultimate penalty of the law as he died in prison before the sentence could be carried out. For Billings and Catherine there would be no such escape, and they were due for execution on Monday 9 May 1726, along with eight other men.

On the morning of the execution, three carts left the prison for Tyburn. In the first cart were Gabriel Lawrence, William Griffin and Thomas Wright, three men who had been sentenced to death for sodomy. In the next, rode John Gillingham, John Mapp and Henry Vigius, three highway-robbers, and in the last cart rode Billings, John Cotterell and James Dupress, two men condemned for burglary. As for Catherine, she was dragged along behind the carts, on a hurdle.

The procession duly arrived at Tyburn, where the three carts were positioned under the beams of the scaffold. The executioner, Richard Arnet, secured each man in turn, put a noose around their necks, and the carts were then removed, leaving them suspended. Catherine was able to watch the death throes of all nine men, including those of her son, Billings. Then it came to her turn to die.

Although the sentence for petty treason was to be burned alive, mercy was invariably shown to such unfortunates. A cord was fastened around the condemned woman's neck, passed through a hole in the stake to which she was tied, and then to the executioner's hand. The custom was that the condemned woman would be strangled before the flames could reach her. Unfortunately, on this occasion, luck was not on Catherine's side.

As Arnet began to pull on the rope, the flames from the burning faggots blew towards his hands, burning them. He had no choice but to let go. Catherine, therefore, was still alive as the flames licked around her.

Three blood-curdling screams echoed around Tyburn as Catherine began to burn. She was seen trying to push the burning faggots away from herself but it was no use. The flames grew ever stronger and Catherine was still alive.

Contemporary reports of the execution claim that Arnet, seeing the distress that Catherine was in, threw a massive piece of wood at her head, which shattered her skull and killed her, putting her out of her misery. Whatever the truth of that, Catherine finally fell silent and, after a full hour, her body was reduced to ashes. As for Billings, his body was later taken down from the scaffold and hanged in chains on the road to Paddington.

# CHAPTER 2

# Catherine Conway, Elizabeth Banks and Margaret Harvey
# 1750

**E**xecutions at Tyburn were a public spectacle, and on occasions many miscreants were hanged at the same time. We have already seen how, in Chapter 1, a total of eleven executions took place on the one day, much to the satisfaction of the mob. Female executions were common, but far less common were multiple executions where all those hanged were female. One such occasion is the subject of this chapter.

### Catherine Conway

Catherine, who was forty-five years of age, had been born in Kilkenny, Ireland. When she was just fourteen, she married Richard, much to the disapproval of her parents. The newly-weds moved to Waterford, where Catherine eventually produced no less than ten children.

Some time around 1743, one of Catherine's sons, a sailor, fell seriously ill at Portsmouth. Catherine and her husband immediately travelled to that city to take care of him but, once he had recovered, they did not return to Ireland but travelled up to Liverpool instead, where two more of their children were now living.

Five years later, in 1748, Catherine received the news that her eldest son, John, had died abroad, whilst serving on a ship. She and her husband then went to London in order to collect any wages that might have been due to him. They had little trouble in collecting the money, most of which was taken by Richard who then spent it on drink and other women. The problem was that this gave Richard an idea about making still more money.

According to the story Catherine would later tell the authorities, Richard had discovered that another sailor, William Noble, had also died on board the same ship that John had served on. Richard suggested to Catherine that she should represent herself as William's mother, draw up a will naming her as beneficiary and then claim the wages due to his estate. After some discussion, Catherine agreed to the plan.

A fake will was drawn up, dated 9 July 1744. After all, it would not do to place a recent date on the forgery in case that aroused suspicion. Catherine and Richard then travelled down to Chatham, presented the will to the naval authorities and, on 2 July 1748, received the sum of £20 1s 6d, being the wages due to William Noble. Once again, Richard pocketed most of the money and then promptly disappeared. Catherine then returned to her family in Liverpool.

The fraud was soon discovered when the real family of William Noble came forward. Catherine was traced to Liverpool, arrested and placed into jail there. Days later, a writ was served which ordered that she be transferred to Newgate, pending her trial for uttering a forged will. That trial took place in April 1749 and, having confessed her guilt, Catherine was duly sentenced to death. As for Richard Conway, the supposed instigator of the crime, he was never traced.

## Margaret Harvey

Margaret was also an Irish girl, having been born in Dublin, in 1725. When she was about sixteen years old, she married John Harvey, at St Patrick's church, also in Dublin.

John earned his living as a sailor and, consequently, spent long periods away from home. A jealous man, he managed to convince himself that, whilst he was at sea, his wife had been seeing other men. Though there was no truth in this, Margaret was unable to convince John that she had been faithful to him and a series of arguments followed. These grew ever more serious and on some occasions, John had even been known to pull a knife on Margaret and cut her about the head.

This situation persisted for some time, until one day, when John was back at sea, a female friend told Margaret that she knew of another man who wanted to be with her. He would treat her fairly and kindly and would support her if only she would leave her husband and live with him. Tired of all the arguments and assaults from her husband, Margaret agreed to move in with the other man.

When John Harvey returned from sea the next time he found that all his suspicions were now proven. His wife was cohabiting with another man. Declaring that he wanted nothing more to do with Margaret, John left Ireland and moved to London.

It wasn't very long before the new man in Margaret's life discarded her. He told her that he had <u>had</u> what he wanted from her and was no longer attracted to her. Since her parents were now dead, Margaret had no one to support her. Somewhat reluctantly, she decided to move to London, try to find her husband, and attempt a reconciliation.

Margaret had no luck in tracing John, so took a position as a servant in Marylebone Street. She did not, however, stay there for very long. One day she spent some time in the company of a group of sailors and some women, where large quantities of drink were consumed. She decided that she had had enough of servitude and vowed never to return to the house, taking lodgings instead in St Giles Pound.

On 14 June 1749, Margaret was again in the company of some sailors and the group went drinking in various establishments around Tower Hill and Wapping. Soon, all were very drunk and one of the sailors then suggested to Margaret that she should relieve a passing gentleman, Robert Lane, of his gold pocket watch. Margaret did steal the watch and chain from Robert, but in her drunken state she was so obvious in her actions that Robert raised the alarm and chased after her. Margaret seemed to be getting away until she turned into Russell Street, off Covent Garden. That street was a cul-de-sac. Margaret was seized there and handed over to the authorities. With the evidence of Robert Lane, there was little difficulty in convicting her of theft, and she too was sentenced to death.

## Elizabeth Banks

Elizabeth had been born in Weymouth, but her parents both died when she was very young. As a result, Elizabeth was taken into the care of the parish, who decided, when she was old enough, to apprentice her to a mistress. This woman treated her very badly and, at the age of ten, Elizabeth ran away, to Dorchester.

The young girl only stayed in Dorchester for a few days before she befriended a wagon driver, who told her that he was travelling to London. Elizabeth persuaded him to give her a lift and was eventually dropped off outside the *Black Bull Inn*, on Piccadilly. The landlady of that public house took an immediate liking to the attractive ten year old and Elizabeth was invited to stay in her house. In fact, she went on to live in comfort there for seven years.

At the age of seventeen, Elizabeth, used to the atmosphere of a public house, took a position in another such establishment, in St Mary Le Strand, where she stayed for four or five years. During that time she married her first husband and together they moved into Russell Court, off Drury Lane, where Elizabeth gave birth to four children. Sadly, over the next few years, Elizabeth's husband and all four of her children died, leaving her alone again.

Elizabeth returned to employment in the licensed trade and worked in various public houses around The Strand. After nine or ten years she married her second husband, but he was only a labourer, making very little money.

On 2 May 1750, a young girl named Frances Mercer was found wandering, in a state of undress. She told those who came to her aid that a woman had stripped her, taken her clothes, placed them into a bundle and walked off with them. The woman was still in the vicinity and was soon arrested. That woman was Elizabeth Banks. She was charged with stealing the child's clothing but, since this had taken place on the King's highway, it was deemed to be highway robbery.

In her defence, Elizabeth claimed that Frances had been with another woman who was carrying a bundle of clothing. The woman said she had to visit someone inside a certain house and offered Elizabeth 2d to watch the child and the bundle. The woman then simply disappeared, and when Elizabeth was arrested she was merely looking for the woman to hand the clothing back. It was a weak story at best, and did nothing to explain how Frances had been found almost naked.

## The Executions

In fact, two other women were also sentenced to death and due to be hanged at the same time. Judith Archer had been found guilty of stealing £28 from a gentleman named William Finch, and Mary Ryan had been sentenced to death for housebreaking; but both had been reprieved, and sentenced to be transported instead. For Catherine Conway, Elizabeth Banks and Margaret Harvey, there was to be no such escape.

On the morning of 6 July 1750, all three women were placed into a cart at Newgate prison and taken to the place of execution at Tyburn. All three seemed, rather naturally, to be deeply distressed, but according to the account of the Ordinary of Newgate, none said anything of merit before the nooses were tied to the triple beam, the cart driven away, and the three women left to strangle slowly to death.

# CHAPTER 3

# Elizabeth Brownrigg
# 1767

Although she loved her step-daughter, there was no way that Mary Clifford could afford to take care of her. Mary had married the child's father in May 1760, but now he had walked out on her, leaving the child behind. The girl, also named Mary, was placed in the care of the parish and Mary senior went to live in Cambridgeshire. By late 1765, the younger Mary Clifford was now some thirteen years of age and facing a somewhat unsure future.

The first duty of the parish officers was to provide a good and stable home for Mary. She appeared to be an intelligent and capable girl and it was suggested that she might be apprenticed to a suitable employer. After due consideration, the authorities decided that the best place for her might be with a well-known and respected midwife, Elizabeth Brownrigg, who lived in Flower-de-Luce Court, which lay off Fetter Lane.

Elizabeth had been born in 1720 and, whilst still a teenager, had married an apprentice plumber, James Brownrigg. By all accounts, their union was a happy enough one and eventually Elizabeth produced no less than sixteen children. Unfortunately, child mortality being what it was, only three of those children had survived for any length of time. By 1766, James Brownrigg was a successful businessman, and his wife Elizabeth had studied midwifery. So capable was she that she had now been appointed as midwife to the workhouse. Their one remaining daughter, Mary, had now left home, leaving two sons, John and William, living at home with their parents.

There was, however, one slight concern with placing the young Mary Clifford with the Brownriggs. Two girls had been placed there previously, and one of these had subsequently run away. Mary Jones had been apprenticed to Mrs Brownrigg in

1765 but had run away after a short time and appeared at the Foundling Hospital, claiming that she had been badly beaten and abused. A letter was sent to James Brownrigg, demanding to know how the child had received the injuries she displayed and stating that action might well be taken against him. James simply ignored the letter and no further action was taken. It was probably nothing but a storm in a teacup so, in early 1766, Mary Clifford was despatched to Elizabeth Brownrigg's care in Fetter Lane.

Less than a year and a half later, Mary Clifford senior returned to London and wished to see her step-daughter who would now be fourteen years old. She knew that Mary junior had been placed with the Brownriggs so, on 12 July, she went to their house and asked to see her step-daughter. To her surprise, the young man who opened the door said that there was no one of that name at the address.

Rather puzzled, Mary went to the authorities and checked that she did have the correct address. Told that she had, Mary returned to Fetter Lane but was given the same story: that there was no child named Mary Clifford at the house. Not one to be deterred, Mary then spoke to some of the neighbours and one, a baker who lived next door to the Brownriggs, said that he would have his own apprentice, William Clipson, keep an eye out for the girl.

William Clipson performed his duties with diligence and his efforts were rewarded on Monday 3 August 1767, when he saw a young girl in the yard of the Brownrigg's house. William called out to her but she either didn't hear him, or chose to ignore him. Eventually, William dropped a small stone, which touched the girl who then looked up towards him. William could see that she sported two black eyes and other injuries, but before he could speak to her, Elizabeth Brownrigg shouted for her to come inside. It did not matter, for William could now prove that there was a young girl inside the house. He took the information to his master who duly passed it on to Mary Clifford senior.

The following day, 4 August, Mary returned to Fetter Lane but this time she had two gentlemen with her: William Grundy, the overseer of the parish of St Dunstan's, and John

Elsdale, the overseer of the precinct of the Whitefriars District. The front door was opened by James Brownrigg himself, and when the two overseers demanded to see the young Mary Clifford, James did not deny her existence but claimed that she was no longer at the house but had gone to live with another family in Stanstead. Told that a young girl had been seen in the yard the previous day, James produced another apprentice, Mary Mitchell, who confirmed her master's story that the other Mary had gone to live in Stanstead. Grundy and Elsdale were not, however, satisfied and continued to question James Brownrigg. Whilst they did so, Elizabeth Brownrigg and her son John, both left the house. Though the two overseers could not know it at the time, both had just escaped from their clutches.

The questioning of James continued, but he persisted in his claim that Mary Clifford was no longer in the house. Grundy and Elsdale then took Mary Mitchell to the workhouse were they could speak to her without James influencing her answers. Told that she was now safe and would not be returning to the Brownrigg's household, Mary Mitchell finally admitted that Mary Clifford was in the house. Grundy and Elsdale returned to Fetter Lane and spoke to James Brownrigg again. He kept to the same story, until the overseers informed him that they were still not satisfied and, if he did not produce Mary, they would be forced to believe that he had done away with her and would face a charge of murder.

A constable was duly called and told to take James into custody. At that point a neighbour, Thomas Coulson, came into the house and, hearing that James was about to be taken to prison, offered to stand bail in the sum of £500. Coulson also sent for a lawyer to offer advice but Grundy and Elsdale were not to be moved. Either James produced the child, or he would be incarcerated and charged. Finally he demurred and Mary Clifford was produced.

None of the men who saw the child could quite believe their eyes. The girl was a mass of bruises and wounds. Her throat and mouth were so badly swollen that she was unable to speak. Coulson carefully sat the child down and asked her who had beaten her to such an extent, but she was unable to form the words to answer him. Coulson decided to try to make things easier. He asked Mary if her master, James, had beaten her. Mary, obviously in extreme pain, managed to utter a long, drawn-out 'No'. Asked then if the beating had been inflicted by her mistress, Elizabeth Brownrigg, Mary managed an equally painful and drawn-out 'Yes'.

Mary was taken into the care of the workhouse whilst James Brownrigg was taken into custody. A warrant was issued for the arrest of Elizabeth and John Brownrigg, and details of their descriptions were published in the newspapers. The following day, Wednesday, 5 August, Mary was taken to St Bartholomew's hospital but, despite medical attention, she died from her injuries on Sunday, 9 August 1767.

Elizabeth and John Brownrigg now moved from lodging to lodging but with half of London looking for them, it was only a matter of time before they were captured. By 15 August, they had taken rooms with a Mr Dunbar in Wandsworth, but that same day, he read a newspaper article about the crime and a description of a woman and boy, who were being sought by the authorities. Later that same day, Elizabeth and John were taken into custody and then, along with James, charged with the murder of poor Mary Clifford.

❦ The trial of the three defendants opened at the Old Bailey, on 9 September. All pleaded not guilty to the charge of wilful murder.

The first, and arguably the most important witness was the other female apprentice, Mary Mitchell, who told the court that she was now almost sixteen years old. Mary had been the very first apprentice in the house, arriving in 1765. Mary Clifford had arrived in mid 1766 and the abuse inflicted upon her had started soon afterwards.

In her time there, Mitchell had seen Elizabeth Brownrigg beat Mary Clifford with a walking cane, a hearth-brush, a riding whip, sticks and other items. Individual events were then referred to.

It appeared that the serious mistreatment had started because Mary Clifford wet her bed. For that reason, she was no longer permitted to sleep upstairs or in the corridors but was despatched to the cellar. She was not fed well and, one day, forced open a cupboard in her search for food. Once Elizabeth Brownrigg discovered this, she forced Mary to strip naked and beat her with the stump of a riding whip.

Elizabeth, however, was not the only one to inflict punishments. On one occasion, John Brownrigg had beaten Mary with the buckle end of a leather strap for not turning up a bed correctly. At the time, Mary had only been wearing a short waistcoat, which did not cover her lower half. In all he struck her eight or ten times, encouraged in his efforts by his mother.

Most of the beatings inflicted by Elizabeth upon Mary Clifford took place in the kitchen and, during these, Mary's hands would be tied together and then fastened in turn to a waste pipe which ran across the ceiling. One day, Elizabeth decided on a slight refinement and had a hook screwed into the ceiling. Now Mary's hands could be tied up to the hook, giving Elizabeth greater flexibility in her beatings.

The blows were struck all over Mary's body, but Elizabeth seemed to concentrate most of her efforts on the head and shoulders. About the only respite came during the weekends, which the Brownriggs often spent in Islington. At that time, the two Marys would be locked in the cellar, often with nothing to eat and no water to drink.

Mary Mitchell then recalled Friday 31 July 1767. Mary Clifford was in reasonable health at that time. Only her shoulders were sore, having by then scabbed over from a previous beating. The Brownriggs went away as usual, but when they returned on the Sunday, Elizabeth claimed that neither of the girls had done any work whilst they were away. Mary Clifford was fastened to the hook in the kitchen and a horse whip was used on her. In all, Mary was tied up some five times that day and on each occasion received blows from the whip. She was kept naked for most of the day, only being allowed to put on a gown and a petticoat at night.

George Benham also lived in the house in Fetter Lane, being an apprentice to James Brownrigg. He had joined the household on 2 December 1766 and saw both the female apprentices beaten on a regular basis, though Mary Clifford always seemed to get the worst of it.

Some of George's evidence was contradictory. In one part, he claimed that he had never seen Mary Clifford tied up or naked, but later referred to an incident when he had been asked, by Elizabeth, to lock Mary in the cellar. At the time, she was only wearing shoes and stockings.

After the three members of the Brownrigg family had been arrested, George went to see his master in prison. James instructed him to go back to the house and remove the hook from the kitchen ceiling. He was also told to burn any sticks he could find. George had done as he was asked. It was George who had answered the door to Mary's step-mother and, again acting on James' instructions, had told her that her daughter was not there.

After Mary Clifford senior had given her evidence, William Clipson told the court how he had seen the beaten girl in the yard on 3 August. His evidence was followed by that of the two overseers, William Grundy and James Elsdale.

William Denbeigh was the apothecary at the workhouse and he testified that Mary Clifford had been placed into his care on 4 August. The top of her head and shoulders were very bloody and when he tried to remove the girl's shift, he found that the material was fused into the wounds upon her body. He removed it as carefully as he could but it caused the girl great pain and caused her wounds to bleed. Once he had removed the shift, Denbeigh saw that Mary was bruised from the top of her head to the bottom of her feet and, in fact, described her body as one continuous sore. It was clear that she needed more expert assistance, so Mary was then transferred to the hospital.

Mr Young was a surgeon at St Bartholomew's Hospital. He testified that Mary was brought to the hospital on 5 August and he had first had care of her on 6 August. Mr Young, in addition to the other injuries, reported a swelling on Mary's neck, consistent with a chain being tied tightly around it. Despite his best efforts, Mary died on 9 August.

The time came for the three defendants to put forward their defences. James Brownrigg said that he would produce witnesses, who would say that he never beat Mary. As for telling the authorities that Mary had gone to Stanstead, he was merely repeating what his wife had told him.

Elizabeth Brownrigg admitted that she had given Mary Clifford several lashes, but claimed that she had no intention of killing the child. As for the marks on Mary's neck, she had fallen down the stairs whilst carrying a saucepan and the handle of it had struck her hard.

John Brownrigg claimed that he had no recollection of any events relating to the dead girl and therefore could put forward no real defence to the charges against him.

Minor witnesses were then called to give evidence as to James Brownrigg's character and to events after the arrest. John Williams, for example, had been visiting a friend in the hospital and saw both girls receiving treatment there. He had asked Mary Mitchell who had hit them and she had told him that Elizabeth and John had beaten them, but James had only ever tapped her once or twice.

John Lucas said he had known James for ten years and always believed him to be an upright and gentle man. Jarvis Reeves, who had known James for between twelve and fifteen years, said much the same, as did Alexander Willes, who had known James for two years.

The jury retired to consider the evidence. When they returned to court with their verdicts, they announced that Elizabeth was guilty as charged, but both James and John were acquitted. They were not, however, free to go. Both men were held in custody and charged with assaulting and abusing Mary Mitchell. As for Elizabeth, she was sentenced to death, her body later to be dissected.

At first, Elizabeth continued to protest her innocence but in due course, she confessed her guilt to the chaplain. On Sunday 13 September, she attended the chapel at Newgate prison, where her husband and son were allowed to be with her. The following morning, Monday 14 September, both men were again allowed to be with Elizabeth as she prayed and received communion. They then made their last farewells in the Press Yard, after which Elizabeth was placed into a cart and escorted to Tyburn.

All along the route, crowds lined the streets hurling abuse, and shouting that she should go straight to Hell. At Tyburn, the Ordinary of Newgate, the Reverend Joseph Moore, sang verses from the fifth psalm before the noose was placed around Elizabeth's neck. Her last words were:

*Lord Jesus, receive my spirit.*

Just over one month later, on 21 October, James and John Brownrigg were found guilty of abusing Mary Mitchell. They were each sentenced to six months' imprisonment and to enter into a recognisance for their good behaviour for the next seven years.

# CHAPTER 4

# Charlotte Gardiner and Mary Roberts
# 1780

I n the late 1660s, a number of severe anti-Catholic Acts were passed, after the restoration of the monarchy. That situation persisted for some years until, in 1778, the Roman Catholic Relief Act reversed much of the previous legislation. That new Act, in its turn, caused a protestant backlash until, eventually, a petition was drawn up by a member of parliament, Lord George Gordon.

Gordon was a retired navy lieutenant and it was Friday 2 June 1780, when he led a crowd estimated at somewhere between 20,000 and 40,000, to the House of Commons, to hand the petition in. To show their support, many members of that crowd wore blue cockades, or carried small blue flags with the legend: 'No Popery!' The petition was presented, but the crowd did not disperse and by that evening, the crowd had become a mob, intent on further action.

The first targets were Catholic churches, whose windows were smashed, doors broken open and furniture removed and burned. Later still, the mob turned their attention to Catholic businesses, and houses. From there, public buildings were targeted including the Bank of England, and three prisons: Newgate, Fleet and the Marshalsea.

Parliament had been slow to act against the rioters, but finally, on Wednesday 7 June, troops were sent in with orders to fire on the mob. In all, some 285 people were killed, 173 wounded and 139 arrested. The final vestiges of the riot would not actually be quelled until Friday 9 July, but to all intents and purposes, the worst of the trouble was over by 7 June, and the trials of those involved could begin.

Somewhat surprisingly, Lord Gordon himself was acquitted of the charge of riot. He continued to act as a member of parliament, though he would later be imprisoned for libel, dying in Newgate prison in 1793. Many of the other rioters were not as fortunate. In all, thirty-five men and three women were sentenced to death. Around half of those were reprieved, including the London hangman, Edward Dennis, who would later be called on to execute the others. Of the three women, only one escaped the hangman's noose. This chapter is the story of the other two: Charlotte Gardiner and Mary Roberts.

John Lebarty was an Italian, who ran a public house and shop from his home in St Catherine's Lane. At one stage, Mary Roberts had lodged next door to Mr Lebarty, but she was noisy and argumentative. Eventually, Mr Lebarty called in the authorities and had her evicted. Mary, however, did not move far, taking fresh lodgings further down the same street. According to later testimony, however, Mary may well have borne a grudge.

The petition was presented to parliament on 2 June. Four days later, on Monday 5 June, when the riot was in full swing, Lebarty said that he had seen Mary Roberts in the street, outside his house, shouting that this was a papist's house and must be pulled down. Further, he claimed that the next evening, Tuesday 6 June, she was back again, making precisely the same threats. By now, Lebarty had grown somewhat concerned for his own safety and left his house, staying in lodgings some distance away. He was, therefore, not at home on the evening of Wednesday 7 June, when the mob smashed the windows of his house, gained entry, forced open the front door and began hurling his belongings into the street. These same belongings were then taken up to Tower Hill where a large bonfire was built and Lebarty's possessions burned. Meanwhile, his house was methodically torn down, until only a broken shell remained.

By the time the government forces had restored order in the area, Lebarty's house was no more, but a number of arrests were made, and neighbours helped in picking out those they

said they had seen destroying the house. In addition to Mary
Roberts, these same neighbours also picked out a black girl,
Charlotte Gardiner, who they said had been one of the
ringleaders. Both women were then charged with riot and
appeared together, before Lord Chief Baron Skynner, on 28
June 1780.

The first witness for the prosecution was John Lebarty
himself who told the court of his earlier arguments with Mary
Roberts, having her evicted from her lodgings and her
subsequent threats to destroy his property. He described her
language as most foul and had little doubt that she intended
to carry out her threats. This is why he had left his home and
sought safe lodgings elsewhere.

He was followed to the stand by Thomas Brumett who lived
next door but one to Lebarty, in St Catherine's Lane. He
testified that during the two days that the house was being
attacked, he saw Mary Roberts carrying away Lebarty's beds,
pillows and bolsters. These were taken to the top of Tower Hill
and thrown onto a large bonfire.

Though Lebarty himself had fled his own home, he had not
bothered to take his servant with him. Fifteen-year-old
Elizabeth Frazer said that she was asleep in bed when the mob
smashed the windows and gained entry. Elizabeth then went
downstairs, to find her master's house full of strangers, but
amongst that crowd were two women. Elizabeth recognised
one as Mary Roberts and, since the other was a black woman,
she had little difficulty in also picking out Charlotte Gardiner.

Elizabeth watched in horror as Charlotte encouraged the
mob to destroy the house crying:

> *More wood for the fire.*
> *Down with it, down with it.*
> *More wood for the fire.*

By now, people were throwing things out of the windows, into
the street, where others picked them up and carried them off
to the bonfire on Tower Hill. As for Mary Roberts, Elizabeth
saw her take a bed outside and drag it up the hill.

Thomas Morris lived in Deptford, but at the time of the riots, he was in St Catherine's Lane. It was around 11.00 pm on 7 June, when he saw people breaking into Mr Lebarty's house. Morris left the area, only to return with an armed officer at around 3.00 am the next morning. They both saw Mary Roberts hanging out of an upstairs window and Morris told the officer to aim his weapon at her in order to intimidate her. It apparently had little effect, for Mary merely shouted that he might, 'Fire and be buggered.' Morris was present when the rioters were finally subdued and heard Mary say, as she was arrested, that she was holding some of Mr Lebarty's property for him.

Letitia Harris lived directly opposite to Mr Lebarty's home and she testified that she had seen Charlotte Gardiner take a bed out of the house, on her shoulders. In all, Gardiner made some thirty to forty trips out of the house, taking things with her up Tower Hill. At one stage, she even took off her shoes and stockings, so that she might work faster.

Elisabeth Jolliffe also lived on the opposite side of St Catherine's Lane and she reported that the mob had arrived outside Lebarty's house at some time between 10.00 pm and 11.00 pm. Once they had broken in, it was Charlotte Gardiner who shouted encouragement to the others, crying out, 'Wood for the fire, damn your eyes. More wood for the fire.'

Charlotte Gardiner could say little in her own defence, but Mary Roberts did her best to avoid her fate. She claimed that she had simply been returning to her lodgings, at about 11.00 pm, when the mob had stopped her and demanded to know if she was a Catholic. When she told them that she was not, they said that she must help them destroy this papist's house or they would suffocate her. Indeed, one man then placed a bolster over her head and tried his best to stop her breathing, so that eventually she was forced to join in, for her own safety.

To support this testimony, Mary called Thomas Buddin, who also lived in St Catherine's Lane. He testified that before Mr Lebarty had left the area, he had deposited many of his personal possessions inside Buddin's home for safekeeping. During the destruction of Lebarty's house, Buddin had seen Mary picking up papers and other personal items and heard her say, 'I will take care of them for Mr Lebarty. When he comes for them, he shall have them.'

The final witness was Mary's sister-in-law, also named Mary Roberts. She said that she had married the prisoner's brother and so had known Mary for some twelve or thirteen years. During that time she had always had a good character and had never been in trouble with the law.

The jury now had to decide on the fate of both women. In the case of Charlotte Gardiner, there could be little doubt as to her guilt, but did Mary Roberts deserve the same fate? Only Lebarty had testified that he had heard her issue threats and she had saved some of his property from destruction. Was that the act of an innocent women, forced into helping the mob, or was it some sort of insurance policy so that she could demonstrate that she was not really a part of what had happened? In the event, the jury chose to believe that she too was guilty and both women were then sentenced to death.

Although Tyburn was the main execution place for London, there were also cases where the condemned were hanged close to where they had committed their crimes. Such was the case with Charlotte and Mary, and indeed, all the rioters condemned to death.

The executions began on Tuesday 11 July 1780, and it was on that date that Charlotte Gardiner and Mary Roberts were hanged, along with William McDonald, on a gallows constructed on Tower Hill, the closest open spot to St Catherine's Lane. On the same day, William Brown was hanged in Bishopsgate Street and William Pateman was hanged in Coleman Street.

Other executions followed. On Wednesday 12 July, James Henry was executed on Holborn Hill. That same day, Richard Roberts and Thomas Taplin met their fate in Bow Street. Enoch Fleming was hanged in Oxford Road on Thursday 13 July. Precisely one week later, on 20 July, James Jackson was hanged in Old Bailey, John Gamble was executed in Bethnal

Green and Samuel Solomons was hanged in Whitechapel. Friday 21 July, saw five executions: George Staples in Coleman Street, Jonathan Stacey in White's Alley, and Benjamin Waters, Thomas Price and James Burns in Old Street. The last two, John Gray and Charles Kent, were hanged together in Bloomsbury Square, on Saturday 22 July.

# CHAPTER 5

# Charlotte Goodall
# 1782

On the afternoon of 8 August 1782, at approximately 4.05 pm., two elderly ladies, Frances Fortescue and Frances Trehearn, left their house to have dinner with a neighbour, Mrs Cotton. At 6.45 pm, however, a servant from another neighbour, Mr Kinder, came to the house to tell the two ladies that they should return home as their house had been ransacked.

The house had indeed been robbed and a large number of items had been taken. Frances Fortescue alone lost goods to the value of an estimated £300, including 30 yards of white satin, 18 yards of figured satin, 18 yards of silk, 12 yards of embroidered white satin, a gold watch and a large quantity of silver items. She also lost five guineas in gold coin.

There had been two servants in the house at the time of the robbery: Charlotte Goodall, who had worked there for some three years, and Elizabeth Steen, known as Betty, who had been there for just over a year. Both ladies had been tied up in their respective bedrooms, but by the time Frances Fortescue arrived home, they had both been released by some of the neighbours who had come to their aid.

Almost immediately, Frances noticed something rather strange about the theft. Only cupboards that had contained something of value had been broken open. It was as if the thieves had known precisely where to look. This was, perhaps, explained away by Charlotte Goodall, who said that she had been forced to show the intruders where the valuables were kept.

There was, however, something else which needed to be explained. Charlotte had told her mistress that she had been sweeping the floor when two or three men burst in, seized her, ordered her to lead them to the valuables, and then tied her up. The other servant, Elizabeth Steen, told a slightly different story. The house had been put up for rent and she told Frances that there had been a knock on the front door. Charlotte had assumed it was someone who had come to look at the house and let a gentleman in. No sooner was he through the door than some other men burst in after him. The more she thought about the matter, the more Frances Fortescue came to believe that one of her servants had conspired with the thieves and, at this stage, her suspicions fell upon Elizabeth.

Both girls were questioned at length by the constables and, finally, Elizabeth said that she would tell the truth. She had indeed been involved in the robbery but it had been at the instigation of Charlotte and a gang she was involved in. That gang included Charlotte's mother, Priscilla Goodall, a man named John Edmonds and two others, John Simpson and his wife Elizabeth. In return for her testimony against the others, Elizabeth Steen was not charged with any offence.

In the event, John and Elizabeth Simpson could not be traced. The others, however, were arrested. Charlotte Goodall was charged with stealing, as was John Edmonds. Charlotte's mother, Priscilla, was charged with aiding them and receiving some of the stolen property. There was also a fourth defendant, Stephen Bouchett, who was indicted for receiving some of the items, knowing them to be stolen. All four were tried before Mr Justice Ashurst, on 11 September 1782.

The first witness was Frances Fortescue, who said that when she returned home on the fateful day, both of her servants were crying. Charlotte had rushed into her arms, saying that she was sorry they had been unable to prevent the robbery. Frances had replied that as long as she had not been hurt, it was of no matter. Frances noticed that there was no sign of any disturbance in Charlotte's room, and the only items that had apparently been taken from her were the two buckles from her shoes.

Joseph Kinder knew the two ladies quite well and had called at their house to see them at around 6.00 pm, on 8 August. He had found the door open and the house in disarray. Going upstairs, he had found both servant girls tied to their bedposts and had released them. After finding out where the two ladies had gone for dinner, Joseph then sent his servant to bring them back.

John Clifford was another neighbour and had gone into the house to assist Mr Kinder, once the robbery had been discovered. The following day, acting on information given to him by Elizabeth Steen, he searched a drain below the sink and found two shoe buckles. These were shown to Frances Fortescue, who identified them as the ones removed from Charlotte's shoes. According to Elizabeth, Charlotte had removed them during the robbery, so that she could say she had been a victim too. They were hidden beneath the bed in her room but once the constables had been called, Charlotte had dumped these down the drain in order to hide the incriminating evidence.

Elizabeth Steen gave testimony, protected as she was now from the consequences of her actions. She told the court that some five months before the robbery she had seen Charlotte break open a chest in her mistresses bedroom and steal some pieces of satin, which she said she would pass on to her mother to pawn. Eventually, it was decided that the house should be robbed properly and it was arranged that it would take place on a day when the two old ladies were going out together. Once Frances had informed Charlotte that she was going to Mrs Cottons, the arrangements were made and it was Elizabeth who went to Priscilla Goodall's house in Kingsland Road, to pass on the information.

Elizabeth and Charlotte were both involved in the robbery and went from room to room with the others, selecting the items to steal. Both were then told to wait a full hour before raising the alarm. They were each given two guineas for their assistance.

Elizabeth Greedy lived with John Edmonds in Priscilla's house in Kingsland Road. She claimed that she knew nothing of the robbery, but on the day it had taken place, John had no money when he left the house at about noon. He returned at around 10.00 pm and seemed to suddenly have a good deal of gold in his possession.

The final witnesses told of various members of the gang selling or pawning some of the stolen items. Walter Roberts was a silversmith, with premises in Bishopsgate Street and he told the court he had purchased a pair of silver tongs and some spoons from Bouchett.

Samuel Stevens was a watchmaker in Whitechapel and Bouchett had visited his premises too, selling a silver spoon. In order to explain these sales, Bouchett claimed that he had had nothing to do with the robbery. He had been out fishing one day and had found a red handkerchief tied into a bundle. The items he sold had been inside and he was therefore guilty of nothing more than selling items he had found.

In the event, all four defendants were adjudged to be guilty. Charlotte and John Edmonds were both sentenced to death. Priscilla was sentenced to be burnt in the hand and then imprisoned for one year. In the event, that punishment was succeeded by a more stringent one, for she was later tried for assisting in the theft of items from Frances Trehearn and sentenced instead to fourteen years' transportation. Bouchett also received the same sentence, and eventually he and Priscilla were sent to North America for those fourteen years.

On 15 October 1782, Charlotte Goodall and John Edmonds were hanged along with eight other men: Peter Verrier, Henry Berthond, William Hones, William Odom, Thomas Gladenboul, John Weatherby, John Lafore and John Graham.

Though she was not to know it, Charlotte earned a place in history on the day she died, for she was the last woman ever to be executed at Tyburn.

# CHAPTER 6

# Elizabeth Taylor
# 1785

As far as Samuel Hooker was concerned, 7 May 1785, was just a normal day. He had spent much of it in his draper's shop in Highgate, serving customers and dealing with stock. He closed the shop at the normal time, locked up the premises as usual, and retired to his bed at some time between 11.00 pm and midnight.

The next morning, Samuel rose after 6.00 am and went downstairs to prepare for the day. Still half asleep, as he walked into the kitchen, he was surprised by how brightly the sun shone into the room. Only then did he see the reason for this unusual brightness; someone had removed four courses of bricks from beneath the window, leaving a large hole through which the sun streamed.

Checking his stock, Samuel found that some £200-worth of goods had been stolen. He made a careful list for the authorities. The thieves, whoever they were, had taken 60 yards of linen cloth, ten linen handkerchiefs, 250 yards of lace, 150 yards of edging, 250 yards of black lace, 2,000 yards of silk ribbon, 30 yards of muslin and two silk handkerchiefs. In addition to the material, they had also taken four silver table spoons, five silver tea spoons, a pair of silver tea tongs, and a silver milk ewer.

The first person Samuel told about the robbery was a neighbour, who assisted him in drawing up the list of the stolen items. Once the list had been made, Samuel called in the local constable, Thomas Seasons, and informed him of the robbery. Constable Seasons immediately concluded that this crime might well have been committed by someone who knew the household routine very well. After all, the removal of the four courses of bricks might well have caused a disturbance.

The thief, or thieves, seemed to be aware that Samuel was a sound sleeper and that his rooms were at the opposite end of the premises. Seasons asked Samuel if there was anyone who had either worked there in the past, or who knew his routine, and who might have committed the robbery.

The only name that Samuel could suggest was that of Elizabeth Taylor. She had worked for Samuel, as a servant, some sixteen months ago. Constable Seasons decided to investigate further.

In due course, Seasons discovered that Elizabeth's brother, Martin, was lodging in the house of one Mary Halloway, at 12 Portpool Lane. Seasons visited those premises on 18 May, and made a thorough search of Martin Taylor's room. Some material was discovered there and various items bore the initials VRW, a mark unique to Samuel Hooker's shop. Samuel had little trouble in identifying the material as his, and Martin was taken into custody.

Later that same day, and acting on information received, Seasons travelled to Bow, where he saw Elizabeth Taylor in the marketplace. As the constable approached, Elizabeth made a dash for freedom. Stalls were knocked over in the ensuing chase and some of the local populace tried to assist Elizabeth by blocking the constable's way but, despite these efforts, Elizabeth too was apprehended.

The trial of Elizabeth Taylor and her brother Martin took place at the Old Bailey before Mr Justice Butler, on 29 June 1785. The case for the prosecution was led by Mr Silvester whilst Mr Garrow led for the defence.

Mary Halloway testified that, at various times, both brother and sister had lodged at her house though, at the time he was taken, only Martin Taylor had rooms there. Mary told of the search made by constable Seasons and the items discovered there. She also said that Martin had given her some of the cloth so that she could make some shifts for Elizabeth.

Constable Seasons said that at the time he had searched Mary Halloway's house, he had found stolen items and, at that stage, was unsure as to whether Mrs Halloway was actively involved in the theft. As a safety measure, he had also arrested her, but subsequent enquiries had shown that Mary Halloway knew nothing of the robbery, and had not known that the items Martin gave her were stolen. As a result, no charges had been preferred against her.

Continuing his evidence, Seasons said that he had also searched the rooms of Mrs Powell, who also lived at 12 Portpool Lane. Other items had been found in her rooms and again, this material had been given to her by Martin Taylor.

Ann Powell confirmed that evidence, saying that Martin had given her some linen and asked her to make two shifts for his wife, Catherine. She also confirmed that both she and Mrs Halloway worked as dressmakers.

Martin Taylor did put forward a defence. He claimed that he had met a man who asked him if he wished to look at some handkerchiefs, with a view to buying them. Martin had agreed and had also looked at some linen. He said that he then bought 14 yards of that linen, at 22 pence per yard, and had then handed it over to Mrs Halloway and Mrs Powell. Martin was not able, however, to name this man, or produce any witnesses to the supposed transaction.

In her defence, Elizabeth Taylor simply claimed that she knew nothing of the robbery. However, when first taken into custody, she had, apparently, made a full confession to the robbery, saying that it had been Martin and another man who removed the bricks from Mr Hooker's house. Martin had then gone inside and passed the items out to her. Now, at her trial, Elizabeth tried to claim that she had been forced into this confession by Constable Seasons, who had told her that if she did not confess, she would certainly hang. It was difficult to accept this claim as, should she now be found guilty, Elizabeth would still face the hangman's noose. In the event, both defendants were indeed found guilty, and sentenced to death.

At 7.30 am, on the morning of Wednesday 17 August 1785, Elizabeth Taylor, her brother Martin, and six other men, were led from their cells at Newgate, into the Press Yard. All had their leg irons and shackles removed, and then had their hands tied in front of them. They were then led across the yard, through the debtor's door, to the waiting gallows outside.

As the eight were led up the steps of the portable gallows, there were cries from the crowd of 'hats off'. This was not, however, a sign of respect for those who were about to die. The cry was merely an exhortation from those at the back who, if hats were not removed, would be unable to get a clear view of the proceedings.

Prayers were then said, by the Ordinary of Newgate, and after these had finished, at around 8.15 am, a signal was given to the executioner who pulled a lever. A trap fell and Elizabeth Taylor, her brother Martin, along with James Lockhart, John Rebouit, John Morris, James Guthrie, Richard Jacobs and Thomas Bailey, dropped the 18 inches or so, until the ropes became taught.

Elizabeth was only the third woman to be executed in public at Newgate, since the closure of the gallows at Tyburn. The first had been Frances Warren, hanged for burglary, on 9 December 1783, whilst the second had been Mary Moody, hanged for theft, on 21 January 1784.

# CHAPTER 7

# Elizabeth Watson
# 1787

Some time at the end of July 1785, a lady walked into a draper's shop on Tower Hill, run by Mr John Wiltshire. She identified herself as Mrs Watson and said that she ran a similar shop in Paradise Street, Rotherhithe, and wished to buy a large quantity of quality Irish cloth.

Mrs Watson then spent a good deal of time examining the best cloth John Wiltshire had available and selected some tablecloths, handkerchiefs and other items, to the value of between £50 and £60 (about £3,300 in today's money). Then, almost as an afterthought, Mrs Watson remembered that she had a customer calling that very afternoon, who also wanted a nice piece of Irish linen. A piece was selected, to the value of fifty shillings (c.£160 today), and Mrs Watson said that she would take this item with her, as she needed to show her own customer later that day.

At first, John Wiltshire was loath to let his new customer take this linen with her. After all, it was the first time she had purchased anything from him, so she had not established a business relationship, which allowed for such credit. Mrs Watson seemed so concerned, though, that she might have to break her promise to her customer and, of course, John did not wish to lose such a valuable order. After much discussion, he allowed Mrs Watson to take the piece of linen, valued at fifty shillings and said he would deliver the rest of the order the next day, when Mrs Watson would settle his bill in full.

The next day, John Wiltshire parcelled up the rest of the order and travelled to Paradise Street. There was no sign of any draper's shop in the area and when John asked local people if they knew of Mrs Watson, none of them did. It seemed that John had been the victim of a fraud and had lost linen worth fifty shillings.

The matter would, no doubt, have rested there but, some six weeks later, John Wiltshire was in Rosemary Lane when he spotted a familiar face: none other than Mrs Watson. He accosted her and demanded to know why she had defrauded him in this way. She begged him not to expose her, saying that she was a mother who had a bad husband and he had forced her into the subterfuge. Mr Wiltshire was not to be moved. He called for a constable and Mrs Watson was taken into custody.

Mrs Watson, subsequently identified as Elizabeth Watson, faced her trial on a charge of fraud, on 19 October 1785. In addition to John Wiltshire, the prosecution also called Francis Holdsworth who lived in Paradise Street. He had been approached by John whilst searching for Mrs Watson's shop, and was able to confirm that he had lived in the area for some considerable time and had never heard of a draper's shop run by a Mrs Watson.

Asked to explain her actions, Elizabeth admitted that she had taken the cloth and had no defence to what she had done. She went on to say that she had given birth to eight children so far and, as the court could plainly see, was now heavily pregnant with the ninth.

Found guilty, Elizabeth was told that normally, a crime such as hers would attract a sentence of at least one year in prison. However, due to her condition and the fact that she had admitted her crime to the court, it was decided to be merciful. She was sentenced to just three months which meant that with the time already served since her arrest, she would be free by the end of November 1785.

Elizabeth, though, did not learn from her brush with the law, for she was back in court on 23 May 1787, charged with an almost identical offence: the theft, by fraud, of goods worth sixty-one shillings, from John Wilkinson.

John Wilkinson ran a draper's shop, specialising in woollens, from Cock Court, Ludgate Hill. On 1 December 1786, Elizabeth Watson walked into his shop and identified herself as the wife of Captain Pearce, who lived at the *King's Head*, Stratford. She went on to explain that there had been a recent death in the family and she would, therefore, require enough grey cloth to make up two mourning coats; one for Captain Pearce and one for his friend.

After some discussion about how much material would be needed, a total of seven yards was agreed upon. Elizabeth then stated that the family had been customers of Mr John Sloan, a tailor, of Johnson's Court, Fleet Street. Mr Sloan had died recently but his widow had agreed to make up the mourning coats and the material should be sent to her establishment. John Wilkinson, of course, knew all about Mr Sloan and this story seemed to confirm in his mind that the sale was a genuine one. For that reason, he raised no argument when Elizabeth went on to say that she wanted some material to make up suits for two boys who were at boarding school. Three and a half yards of suitable material, valued at sixty-one shillings, was then selected, parcelled up, and taken by Elizabeth to a waiting coach on Ludgate Hill.

Naturally, when arrangements were made to deliver the rest of the material, and the bill for the whole order, to Ann Sloan, the tailor's widow, she knew nothing of it. Nor had she ever heard of a Captain Pearce, who was supposed to be one of her husband's customers.

Elizabeth Watson had, however, made a number of rather fundamental mistakes. First, she had committed a similar offence less than two years before. Secondly, she had once lodged with Thomas Blackburne, who lived at Stratford. Although he was now a carpenter by trade, he had once been the constable of the district and, when the police began searching the area, looking for the miscreant, he was able to confirm that the description of the customer served by John Wilkinson, matched that of Elizabeth Watson.

Elizabeth was traced, arrested, and placed on trial again. John Wilkinson positively identified her as the woman who had defrauded him out of the three and a half yards of material. Other witnesses were then called, including William Bantock, who had lived at Stratford for seventeen years and confirmed that no gentleman named Captain Pearce had ever lived in the area. This was also confirmed by John Batt, the landlord of the *King's Head*.

In her defence, Elizabeth simply claimed that she was not the woman who had gone into John Wilkinson's shop and stolen the material. She was not believed and a guilty verdict was returned. Before sentence was passed the judge explained:

> *I am extremely sorry that your conduct puts it out of the power of the Court, to show you that leniency that they might otherwise incline to do. You are the same person who about two years ago was sentenced to be imprisoned for six months. It is the duty of the Court on a second conviction, certainly to pass a severer sentence than that of the first.*

Elizabeth Watson was then sentenced to be transported, for a term of seven years.

# CHAPTER 8

# Mary Finlayson
# 1795

ohn Gibbs was a sailor, his ship being called *The Lightning*, and in early November 1794, that vessel, back from a voyage to Jamaica, docked along the River Thames, and Gibbs took some well deserved shore leave in London.

Early on the morning of Sunday 9 November, Gibbs left a public house close to King James' Stairs and began to make his way back to his lodgings in Parlour Street. As the sailor approached the foot of Foxes Lane, a heavily-built man came up behind him and pinned Gibbs' arms to his side. As Gibbs struggled, a woman approached and began to rifle through his pockets. She eventually stole a silver watch, a steel watch chain, a cornelian seal set in brass, a steel watch key, a clasp knife and a tin japanned tobacco box. More importantly, perhaps, she also stole 34 guineas in gold.

Satisfied that she had taken everything of value, the woman signalled to her accomplice who then pushed Gibbs to the ground. Then, as if to add insult to injury, the man stole Gibbs' new hat and replaced it with his own shabby one. The couple then made good their escape.

The following morning, Monday 10 November, Gibbs went to the police office in Shadwell to report the assault and theft and there, in *The Virginia Planters*, a public house opposite, he saw a woman who he believed was the same one who had robbed him the previous morning. The man, of course, had approached him from behind and Gibbs had never even seen his face, but he had had a good look at the woman, as she rifled through his pockets and was convinced that this was the same one.

The woman was taken into custody, on Gibbs' identification, and charged accordingly. Her name was Mary Finlayson and her case was heard at the Middlesex Assizes, on 8 December 1794.

One of the first witnesses was a watchman named Jones. At some time between 2.00 am and 3.00 am, on Sunday 9 November, he had been on patrol, when he heard a good deal of noise coming from the area at the foot of Foxes Lane. Going to investigate he found a man and a woman making a lot of noise, having been ejected from a public house named *The Jolly Sailor*.

Jones ordered the woman to be quiet and was greeted with a good deal of verbal abuse. At one stage, the woman offered him a handful of gold if he would go away and leave her alone. Satisfied that there was no other course of action open to him, Jones then called for a constable.

It was Constable John Thomas who came to Jones' aid, but even as the officer approached, the woman placed the coins into her mouth. This was a strange thing to do, and Thomas ordered her to spit the coins into his hand. Thomas then searched the woman and found that in all, she had 13 guineas in gold on her person, along with a half crown piece and a shilling. The woman, who identified herself as thirty-nine-year-old Mary Finlayson, was then taken to the watch-house and locked up for the night.

The next morning, at 10.00 am, Mary was released from custody and asked to explain where she had obtained so much money. She claimed that her brother in Berwick had sent her ten guineas and the rest she had earned from a woman in labour whom she had assisted. Constable Thomas then took Mary back to *The Virginia Planters*, where he asked the landlord to take care of her. Meanwhile, Mary was informed that if she appeared before the justices the next morning, and was able to prove her story, then the rest of her money would be returned to her.

She had indeed appeared before the magistrates the next morning but it had not been to recover her property for by then she had been identified by John Gibbs, and charged with highway robbery. Constable Thomas finished his evidence by explaining that he had held on to the money, which he had found on Mary, apart from one guinea, which he had handed over to John Gibbs so that he might pay for his board and lodgings. This, surely, was highly improper behaviour, as the property had not, by that stage, been shown to belong to him.

The testimony of these two witnesses should also have raised a good deal of doubt. John Gibbs had claimed that he was assaulted and robbed at about 3.00 am. The time of Mary's arrest had been some time between 2.00 am and 3.00 am. There could, of course, have been some discrepancy in the timings, but the circumstances certainly did not agree with the story John Gibbs had told. Mary was in custody by 3.00 am at the very latest and, if the watchman, Jones and Constable Thomas had come upon the scene much before this, why was Mary still at the scene of the robbery? Gibbs himself had said that the couple ran away after robbing him. It is just as likely that Mary was actually in custody at the time John Gibbs was robbed.

The time came for Mary's story to be detailed in court. When she was arrested, she had said that at around 1.00 am, she was heading home, somewhat the worse for drink, when she met the watchman, Jones. At the time she had around 14 guineas on her and Jones took her back to the watch-house, as he believed she was too drunk to be left to her own devices. At the watch-house he had found out about the money and said that if she gave it to him, he would let her go. When she refused, he had called the constable who took her into custody. If this story were true, then Mary was locked up a good two hours before Gibbs was attacked.

It all came down to who the court chose to believe. Ignoring the discrepancies over the time of the robbery, they found Mary guilty as charged. Sentenced to death, Mary Finlayson was hanged on 1 April 1795, alongside William Ball, who had been sentenced to death for forgery.

Mary may well have been innocent of the charge that claimed her life, but she did earn a small place in criminal history. She was the last woman ever to be executed for highway robbery.

# CHAPTER 9

# Anne Hurle
## 1804

Jane Hurle had worked as a housekeeper for Mr Benjamin Allin for some twelve years. That gentleman was housebound and had been confined to his house at Greenwich for more than forty years. He saw very few people and, over the years, grew to trust and rely on Jane more and more. Indeed, by the year 1803, he had come to grant her power of attorney and she handled many of his business and investment affairs.

Some time before Michaelmas 1803, a visitor arrived at Benjamin Allin's house. Anne Hurle was Jane's niece and she was made welcome as a guest. She did not, however, stay for very long, for Anne had plans she wished to put into action.

On Saturday 10 December, Anne called at the offices of George Francillon, a stockbroker who traded from the coffee-house at the Bank of England. Anne explained to Mr Francillon that she wished him to draw up a power of attorney for the transfer of £500 worth of Bank of England three percent stock, from Mr Allin to herself.

Anne explained that her aunt had been the housekeeper to Mr Allin for many years and she had been brought up in his house and had provided him with many years faithful service herself. Mr Allin had decided that she should be rewarded for this service and had decided to give her the stock as a thank you. Mr Francillon duly drew up the document and handed it over to her that same day.

A few days later, on Monday 12 December, Anne returned to Mr Francillon with the document duly signed and witnessed. Anne said that she wished to either sell the stock, or have it transferred into her name as soon as possible. Mr Francillon informed her that he would need to have the document verified and proved by his colleagues before he could execute it for her. Anne was asked to wait whilst this was done.

After some twenty minutes or so, Mr Francillon went to the Bank's proving office to enquire if the document was ready. Mr Thomas Bateman, the clerk who worked there informed him that he would need to speak to him and Miss Hurle and both then went into his private office.

Mr Bateman explained that the signature on the document, purporting to be that of Mr Allin, differed appreciably from the one they had on record at the bank. Mr Bateman asked Francillon if he knew Mr Allin personally and when he said he did not, Bateman turned to Anne Hurle and asked her how she knew him. Anne explained that she had known the old gentleman since she was a child and had been raised in his house. Mr Allin was now close to ninety years of age and in rather poor health, and this might well explain the difference in his signature; however, if there were any doubts, she would be happy to get a new power of attorney signed by Mr Allin and bring that in for consideration.

Mr Bateman said that it would be a great pity to put Miss Hurle to all that extra expense and time and, by coincidence, he happened to know one of the two witnesses who had also signed the document, a Mr Peter Verney. A memorandum was written at the bottom of the document and Bateman then handed it back to Miss Hurle, stating that she should get Mr Verney to sign it and then return the document to his office.

As Mr Francillon and Anne Hurle left the office, she began to tell him a rather different story about her history. Anne now explained that she was a married woman, whereupon Francillon told her that the document was now of no use as, by law, it had to be made out in her married name. Thinking quickly, Anne then said that her marriage had not been a good one. She had met her husband, a man named James Innis, at Bristol and married him there after knowing him just a few days.

Growing ever more curious and suspicious, Francillon then asked Anne which church she had been married in, but she claimed that they had wed in a private house. However, within two hours of the ceremony, Innis had left her, taking most of her property with him and soon afterwards she had discovered that he was already married.

Anne went off back to Greenwich, ostensibly to get the document signed again by Peter Verney. By now, Mr Francillon was far from satisfied, and so went to visit the offices of Owen and Hicks, the firm of solicitors who acted for Mr Allin. What he learned there made him sure that Anne Hurle was attempting to issue a forged document so, when she returned to his office the following morning, Tuesday 13 December, Mr Francillon explained that he would be unable to prove the document that day and she should return the next morning. Mr Francillon then went to Mr Allin's house at Greenwich, taking the power of attorney with him.

When Anne Hurle returned to Mr Francillon's office, on Wednesday morning, she was taken into custody and charged with forging the letter, publishing a forged deed and two counts of attempting to defraud Benjamin Allin.

Anne Hurle faced her trial at the Old Bailey on 11 January 1804, before Sir Archibald Knight. Mr Garrow led for the prosecution, whilst Anne was defended by Mr Knapp.

After Mr Francillon had given his evidence, the court called Thomas Bateman, the inspector of documents such as the power of attorney. He testified that after telling Ann Hurle of the differing signature on the document she had presented, he pointed out to her that he knew Mr Verney, who worked as a cheesemonger, in Greenwich. Mr Verney was also holder of a considerable amount of Bank of England stock and the two men had had business dealings before. Mr Bateman was of the opinion that Mr Verney's signature was also false.

Although he was almost ninety, Mr Benjamin Allin was the next person to step into the witness box. He confirmed that he lived at Greenwich and had, for some years, employed Jane Hurle as his housekeeper. Shown the document produced by Anne Hurle, Mr Allin was able to confirm that it was not his signature at the foot. Further, the document was signed in full, that is, 'Benjamin Allin', and he had not signed his name in that manner for many years. Finally, Mr Allin was able to say that he did not know the two men whose signatures appeared as witnesses to his own.

The first of those signatories was Peter Verney. He told the court that he did know the prisoner, but only as a customer at his shop. He had never met Mr Allin, and had certainly not witnessed that gentleman's signature on a power of attorney. Indeed, his own signature on that document, was false.

The other supposed witness to Mr Allin's signature was Thomas Noulden, a carpenter. He too swore that the signature on the document was not his and he had never met Mr Allin before. He did, however, know the prisoner as Thomas was her godfather.

The final witness was Jane Hurle, the prisoner's aunt. She confirmed that if any documents ever needed to be signed by Mr Allin, it was she who would hand them over to him and then deal with them. The writing on the power of attorney was similar to her employer's but Jane was unable to swear that it was actually his. In any event, she had certainly not given it to him for signature and the first time she had seen the document was when Mr Francillon called at the house and showed it to her.

The verdict was little more than a formality. Anne Hurle had made a rather clumsy attempt to defraud Mr Allin out of £500 (over £16,000 in today's money). Found guilty on all charges, the sentence was deferred until 17 January 1804. On that date, Anne claimed that she was 'with child', but she did not state this with any conviction, and there was not even an examination before this claim was dismissed. Anne was then sentenced to death.

There was to be no reprieve and Anne was sent to Newgate prison to await her fate. There, on Wednesday 8 February 1804, she was hanged in public, outside the prison walls, alongside Methuselah Spalding, who had been sentenced to death for sodomy. Anne was just twenty-two years old.

# CHAPTER 10

# Sarah Puryer
## 1810

Although Sarah lived with John Puryer as his wife, their relationship was rather more complex than that, for Sarah was actually married to John's brother. That relationship had ended and Sarah had now moved in with her brother-in-law at his home in French Gardens. The couple then lived together for a number of years and had five children together, two of whom survived beyond infancy.

Sarah and John did not, however, live happily together. There were many arguments, some of them fuelled by drink, and both seemed to have something of a temper. These arguments came to a head, apparently, on Friday 30 March 1810.

It was on that day that John arrived home, much the worse for drink. Yet another argument followed and though there were no witnesses for what actually passed between the couple, Sarah would later say that at the height of the row, John had thrown her down a flight of stairs. Not content to simply take this punishment, Sarah then went back upstairs to continue the heated discussion. The argument grew ever more desperate until, according to John, she took a lighted candle from its holder and thrust it into his left eye. This was then followed by Sarah hurling a mallet at John, which struck him on the back of the head, causing quite a nasty injury.

On the day after this argument, Saturday 31 March, John Puryer was in Whitechapel market and it was there that he saw an old friend, Mary Reeves. John told Mary about the argument and explained that at the time Sarah had attacked him he was in bed, trying to get to sleep, implying perhaps that he was innocent of any act of incitement.

For the next few days, little was seen of John Puryer but then, on Monday 9 April, one of his sisters-in-law went to see Dr James Crockford and explained that John appeared to be seriously ill and needed to be admitted to hospital. Dr Crockford did go to visit John and said that he would need to be seen by a colleague, Mr Weston, a surgeon.

The treatment John Puryer then received is, perhaps, indicative of the state of medical knowledge at this time. That same day, despite his sickness, John walked to Mr Weston's house and explained, with much difficulty, that he could not open his mouth properly and had been sent there by Dr Crockford. Mr Weston examined John, found a contused wound on the back of his head and concluded that he was almost certainly suffering from lockjaw. Explaining to John that his life was in danger, Mr Weston then wrote a letter to Mr Ashley Cooper at Guy's Hospital and told John to take it to that gentleman without delay.

Still seriously ill, John Puryer struggled to the hospital with his letter of admittance from Mr Weston. Once there, John found that Mr Cooper was not there, but his servant read the letter and then asked him to come back on Friday 13 April, six days from then.

Growing worse all the time, John made the painful journey back to Mr Weston and explained that Mr Cooper wasn't there; and that his servant had said that he should come back in six days. Mr Weston was astounded and explained to John that if he did not gain admission to the hospital, and treatment within hours, he would certainly die. John Puryer did not return to Guy's Hospital, though. His strength barely carried him back to his home in French Gardens, and it was there, in the early hours of Tuesday 10 April, that he passed away.

Forty-five-year-old Sarah Puryer was immediately arrested and charged with murder. She appeared before Mr Justice Grose, on 6 June, to answer that charge and explained to the court that she had only acted in self-defence. John had come home very drunk on that fateful day at the end of March, had thrown her down the stairs and she was afraid that his assault on her would continue. The incident with the candle had been an accident, caused through the struggle, and when she had thrown the mallet, she had not intended to cause him any serious injury, let alone kill him.

Sarah called no fewer than three character witnesses who all confirmed that she was usually a most dutiful wife and mother. This, apparently, did have the desired effect, for Sarah was adjudged to be not guilty of murder, though the jury did find her guilty of manslaughter.

Had she been found guilty of murder, Sarah would, of course, have faced the death penalty. As it was, she might well have faced a lengthy prison sentence, but it appears that the judge, too, believed that there had been a good deal of provocation from the dead man. Thus, Sarah Puryer escaped with the relatively light sentence of just two months in Newgate gaol.

# CHAPTER 11

# Charlotte Newman
# 1817

The constables were growing rather worried. Someone had been passing forged £1 notes in the area around Drury Lane. A number of such notes had been found and, from speaking to the shopkeepers, officers discovered that they had all been passed by a woman. True, she was usually in the company of a man, or occasionally another woman, but it was always the same woman who handed the notes over. Usually she would make a small purchase and get change in the form of silver and copper coins.

A description of the woman was circulated and all constables were told to be on the look-out for her. It was this description, which caused Constable Charles Jeffries to follow a woman, on Saturday 25 October 1817.

The woman was with a young man and Jeffries saw them walking, arm in arm, down Bunhill Row, just after 7.00 pm. Jeffries followed the couple, from a discrete distance, taking great care not to be seen. He followed them down Chiswell Street and saw them enter a wine vault close to St Andrew's church. Looking through the window, Constable Jeffries saw them enjoy a drink together, but did not see any money change hands. In due course, the couple came out of the bar and, after a brief conversation, they parted and walked off in different directions. Since reports said that it was always a female who passed the forged notes, Jeffries decided to follow the woman.

She then walked down Oxford Street and on into Wardour Street. Continuing her journey, she turned into Silver Street and Jeffries saw her go into number 37. Some minutes later, the man who had been with her earlier, also entered 37 Silver Street and Jeffries continued to keep watch from outside.

After some time, the man and woman left the house together and walked on to the *Buck's Head* public house in Carnaby Street. Although he watched the couple from outside, Jeffries saw no money change hands but, after they left the pub, Jeffries went inside and spoke to the landlord, William Soul. He confirmed that the woman had purchased drinks with a £1 note. Jeffries asked to see the note and told Soul that he would need to confiscate it, as he believed it to be a forgery. Unfortunately, by the time he left the *Buck's Head*, there was no sign of the woman, who had handed over the banknote.

A few days later, on Wednesday 29 October, Constable Samuel Plank saw a man and woman who fitted the description given by Constable Jeffries, also in Bunhill Row. He too decided to follow them and much the same story unfolded. The couple went into a public house before walking on to Whitecross Street. From there, they entered another drinking establishment on Holborn Hill, followed by two more in St Giles. No banknotes were handed over in either establishment, and it was not until Plank followed them to the Vine Vaults in Long Acre, that he finally saw a £1 note being handed over to the landlord, William Winkfield. As the pair left the bar, Constable Plank identified himself to Mr Winkfield and asked to see the note the woman had tendered. This too appeared to be a forgery and Plank left the bar immediately in order to follow his quarry. He managed to keep them in sight as far as Smithfield but lost them in the crowds there.

Both constables had followed a woman who had been in the company of a man and who had then handed forged £1 notes to publicans. It did not go unnoticed either, that on both occasions, the woman had been seen initially in the Bunhill Row area. It seemed reasonable to assume, therefore, that her base was in that area, so a special watch was kept there.

On Saturday 1 November, both Constable Plank and Constable Jeffries were on duty in Bunhill Row when they saw the same man and woman. The couple were followed down Whitecross Street, onto Holborn Hill and finally to Denmark Street. It was there that the woman went into a shop shoe on the corner, whilst the man stayed outside as if

on watch. This time, the constables were determined that
their suspects would not escape. Constable Jeffries
immediately took the man into custody whilst Constable
Plank entered the shop.

The woman was sitting on a low stool and asking to see a
pair of ladies boots. As the proprietor's wife, Sarah Bartlett,
attended to her customer, Constable Plank took the owner,
John Bartlett, to one side and said he was a police officer
investigating the passing of forged banknotes. Even as he
spoke, Mrs Bartlett came to the counter with a £1 note, which
the woman customer had handed her. Without delay,
Constable Plank took possession of the note and arrested the
woman on a charge of forgery.

At the police station, the two prisoners readily gave their
identities as Charlotte Newman and George Mansfield,
though neither was prepared to tell the officers where they
lived. However, when they were searched, two identical latch
keys were found, one on each of the suspects. Again returning
to the belief that there was a connection with Bunhill Row, the
keys were taken to that area and tested on the doors. In due
course, it was discovered that the keys fitted the front door of
number 52. That house was owned by Mrs Goodman, who
confirmed that Charlotte Newman did have rooms there.
Those rooms were then searched and a further twenty-eight
£1 notes were discovered.

Charlotte Newman and George Mansfield faced their trial
on 3 December 1817. The initial charges were of producing
forged currency and of passing such a forged note to William
Winkfield, on 29 October.

The first witness was William Winkfield himself. He told the
court that at approximately 8.00 pm, Charlotte Newman had
come into his establishment, in the company of a man. She
had asked for a quart of liquor, the price of which was 4d. She
tendered a £1 note, numbered 27810 and dated 8 February
1817. Asked to sign the note on the back, Charlotte signed it
in the name of Mrs Hughes, of 6 Grub Street. As soon as the
couple had left the premises, Constable Plank had entered,
identified himself as a police officer, and taken the note as
evidence.

After Constable Plank had given his evidence, the prosecution called John Lees, a gentleman who worked for the Bank of England as an inspector of notes. He confirmed that the note Charlotte had handed to William Winkfield was a forgery.

The next two witnesses were John Bartlett and his wife Sarah, who gave evidence of Charlotte seeking to purchase a pair of boots and offering a £1 note in payment. On this occasion, Charlotte had signed the note in the name of Mrs Brown of Brownlow Street.

William Avis was another publican who ran a wine vault from 123 Drury Lane. On 13 October, Charlotte, in the company of another woman, had entered his premises and ordered two glasses of beer. Again, she paid with a £1 note which she endorsed on the back with the name 'Mrs Brown' and the address, King Street.

William Soul was the owner of the *Buck's Head* in Carnaby Street. Charlotte had been in his establishment on 25 October and ordered a quart of gin and a pot of beer, which came to 6d. Another £1 note was offered, this time signed Mrs Brown of 5 Pulteney Street. This transaction was confirmed by William's wife, Ann Soul.

After Constable Jeffries had detailed his sighting and subsequent tailing of Charlotte and George, and of the latter's arrest on 1 November, another officer, Constable John Foy, was called to the stand. He had been with Constable Plank when Charlotte's rooms at 52 Bunhill Row were searched and had witnessed the finding of the twenty-eight £1 notes.

George Clayton was another lodger at 52 Bunhill Row. He was able to confirm that Charlotte had lived there for some four or five months but that whilst George Mansfield was a regular visitor, he did not actually live there.

John Lees from the Bank of England was then recalled. He had examined all the banknotes in this case and was able to confirm that all were forgeries. All the banknotes bore different serial numbers and his examination showed that they were manufactured from two different plates.

Asked to speak in their own defence, Charlotte Newman said: 'The other prisoner is perfectly innocent and knows nothing of this transaction.' George Mansfield said that although he knew Charlotte well, he had no idea that she was passing forged currency and had only gone along with her because she had asked him to. The jury chose to believe this, returning a not guilty verdict on George, but finding Charlotte guilty as charged. She was then sentenced to death.

As soon as the proceedings had ended, the next case was yet another indictment on the same two prisoners. This, of course, had merely been a secondary charge in case the first case had collapsed. Now that Charlotte had received a death sentence, no evidence was offered in this second case and formal not guilty verdicts returned on both prisoners. George Mansfield was then told that he was a free man.

On 17 February 1818, Charlotte Newman was hanged outside Newgate. At the same time, two others: Mary Ann Jones and William Hatchman were also hanged for forgery; and John Attel was hanged for burglary.

# CHAPTER 12

# Ann Mary Chapman
# 1829

At around 6.45 pm, on Wednesday 3 June 1829, Thomas Nelhams, a local farmer, was walking across a field in Turnham Green, with a friend of his, when he thought he heard a faint cry, which sounded like the bleating of a lamb. The sound appeared to come from a ditch at the edge of the field and Thomas walked over to see what had actually caused the sound.

Arriving at the ditch, Thomas looked down and saw a piece of flannel material, largely covered over with grass and weeds. Even as he looked, the material moved and, investigating more closely, Thomas saw that there was a child beneath the material.

Pulling away some of the grass, Thomas saw that the child was lying on its back. It appeared to be in some distress, for its face was a deep black colour, as were the tips of the child's fingers. Thomas left his friend, George, to watch over the child whilst he ran back across the field to the home of Constable Williamson.

Constable John Williamson timed Thomas Nelhams, arrival at a few minutes to 7.00 pm. Having listened to Thomas' story, Williamson then accompanied him back to the ditch where George still stood guard. The constable then took the child out of the ditch and ran, as fast as he could, back to his house where he handed the baby to a local woman with instructions to place the child in warm water.

The baby was quickly undressed, revealing that it was in fact a girl, probably aged about three weeks or so. The warm water began to wash some of the dirt off the child's face and upper body and only now, to his horror, did Williamson realise that beneath the dirt, the child had a black ribbon tied quite tightly around its throat. Wasting no time, Williamson cut through the ribbon, with some difficulty. Almost immediately, the baby took a deep breath and colour began to return to her cheeks. A doctor was called to examine the baby but it appeared that her life was no longer in danger and slowly she grew stronger.

It seemed reasonable to assume that whoever had dumped the baby in the ditch had to know the area quite well. There was a public footpath across the field where she had been found, but only those who knew the area well would know of it. There was also the fact that the ditch was a few hundred yards from that footpath. The miscreant must have known that people rarely strayed from the path, again indicating that he or she knew the area well.

Constable Williamson began his investigation and two important witnesses soon came forward. The first of these was Hannah Dunford, who lived at the *Red Lion* public house in Acton. She told Constable Williamson that at around 5.00 pm on 3 June, she had seen a woman in the tap room. The woman had had two young children with her; one about two or three years old and the other a baby who appeared to be newly born. The woman had had some beer and had also bought a glass of peppermint, which she offered to both the children. She had only stayed a few minutes and left some time after 5.00 pm.

Williamson now believed that he was looking for a woman, who was possibly local, but he still did not have a name for her. This problem was solved when the second witness, Joseph Shepherd, came forward.

Shepherd said that he had seen the woman between 1.00 pm and 2.00 pm, walking up Green Lane, Acton. She had two children with her, both of which she carried. As Shepherd watched, the woman went into the bottom end of a large wheat field and sat down upon the ground. She then took a black ribbon from around her shoulders and looked around to see if anyone might be watching her. Only then did she see Shepherd looking at her from a hole in the edge. The woman then quickly put the ribbon back around her shoulders as he climbed over the gate and joined her in the field.

The two fell into conversation, during which she said that the youngest child was not hers. They walked on together along the pathway, with Shepherd carrying the eldest child for her. At another gate they parted and the woman said that she would wait there for the baby's mother. It was then around 3.00 pm or perhaps a little later.

Shepherd, though, had one more crucial piece of evidence to impart. He had known the woman for some two or three years. She lived elsewhere now but a few years back had worked in East Acton. Her name was Ann Mary Chapman.

A warrant was now drawn up for the arrest of Ann Chapman on a charge of attempted murder. Further investigations showed that until fairly recently she had been an inmate of St George's workhouse in Hanover Square, which was some distance from Acton. It was at that establishment that Constable Williamson interviewed two more witnesses.

Elizabeth Tyler was a nurse at the workhouse and she confirmed that Ann Chapman had been admitted so that she might have her child there. The child was born on 13 May and christened Elizabeth Chapman. Mother and child remained at the workhouse until 2 June, when they were discharged. Another of the inmates, Robert Gay, had been instructed to help Ann with the children, and escort her to her lodgings.

Robert Gay was the second witness Williamson spoke to. Robert said that on 2 June he had carried the children for Ann, and together they had travelled as far as *The Swan Inn* at Bayswater where they had paused for a drink together. From there, they went on as far as Notting Hill, where she said that he need not take her any further as her brother would be meeting her there. By the time Robert left her, with the two children, it was around 8.35 pm.

In fact, it took Constable Williamson a few more days to trace Ann Chapman. It was not until Saturday 6 June, at around 8.30 pm, that he saw her in the company of a man in Hammersmith. Williamson stopped them both and said to Ann, 'I want you. I have been looking for you for a good while. Your name is Ann Chapman.'

Ann replied, 'It is and what of it?' Williamson then informed her that he held a warrant for her arrest, for attempting to murder her child. She denied any involvement, but admitted that she had recently given birth to a baby but it had died and was already buried. Questioned further, Ann went on to deny that she had been at Acton on 3 June and, in fact, had not been in that area for a number of years.

Constable Williamson was, of course, far from satisfied and informed Ann that she would be taken into custody pending further investigations. The young man with her, who identified himself as Matthew Varney, might also be involved, so he too was arrested.

Both prisoners were escorted back to Acton, where Ann was deposited into a private room at *The George* public house. Both Joseph Shepherd and Hannah Dunford were then called in and both made a positive identification. Ann Chapman was the woman they had both seen in Acton on 3 June.

Matthew Varney was then searched and Constable Williamson found a key on his person. By now, Williamson had come to believe that Varney had not been involved in the attempt upon the life of Elizabeth Chapman and, for his part, Varney seemed keen to help the officer in his enquiries. Varney volunteered that the key was to the lodgings he shared with Ann, in Starch Green. Whilst both Ann and Varney remained in custody, Constable Williamson went to search their lodgings. It was there that he found the other child, safe and well.

Back at Acton, and faced with the evidence against her, Ann Chapman finally admitted that she had been the woman who deposited the baby in the ditch. She claimed that she thought someone would find it and give it a better life than she ever could, but this did not explain why she had tied the black ribbon so tightly around the child's neck and hidden it so well in the ditch. Later, she made a further statement which, perhaps, gave more insight into why she had tried to kill her new-born daughter. In that, Ann said that after the child had been born in the workhouse, Varney had come to visit her. He had looked at the child and announced, 'This is not my child. It is not like me.' He also offered violence to the baby and she perhaps felt that if she kept Elizabeth, she would lose her lover.

The trial of Ann Mary Chapman took place on 11 June 1829. She actually faced four charges, which included attempting to strangle Elizabeth and to suffocate her, but the basic charge was that of attempted murder.

After Thomas Nelhams and Constable Williamson had given their testimony, the court heard from Dr John Salter, who had been called to Williamson's house to examine the child. He had little doubt that had the child not been found when she was, she would certainly have died from strangulation. He was unable to say how much longer Elizabeth might have lived, but it would not have been very long.

After Joseph Shepherd, Hannah Dunford, Robert Gay and Elizabeth Tyler, the nurse, had given their testimony, Matthew Varney, Ann's paramour, was called. No charges had been made against him and he was now called as a character witness for Ann. He told the court that he had known Ann since the previous August, and they had lived together as man and wife since that time. Though she was only twenty-eight years old, he knew that Ann had given birth to no less than eight children. She appeared to be a good mother and was always kind to the other child found in their lodgings.

In the event, the verdict, when it came, was that Ann was guilty of attempted murder. She was recommended to mercy, on account of the infant's life having been spared. Nevertheless, the sentence was that she be hanged by the neck, until she was dead.

There was no reprieve, and on 22 July 1829, Ann Mary Chapman was hanged outside Newgate prison alongside six men: Edward Turner, Thomas Crowther, Charles Jones, Edward Martelli, James Butler and Henry Conway.

Though the death sentence for attempted murder remained on the statute books until 1861, and others did suffer hanging for that offence, Ann Chapman was the last woman to be hanged in London for any offence other than murder itself.

# CHAPTER 13

# Martha Browning
## 1846

At approximately 7.45 am, on Monday 1 December 1745, Ann Gaze heard a strident knocking at her front door, at 1 Providence Place, Brewers Green, Westminster. Going to answer it, she found that the caller was Martha Browning, a woman who lived with Ann's mother, sixty-year-old Elizabeth Mundell, at 11 Rochester Street, also in Westminster.

A somewhat breathless Martha explained that Elizabeth had been taken ill that morning, at about 7.00 am, and was now very poorly indeed. Ann Gaze wasted no time in accompanying Martha back to Rochester Street. What she found there, puzzled her a good deal.

Elizabeth Mundell was not, as might be expected, lying in her bed. Indeed, three heavy chairs had been piled up on Elizabeth's bed. Ann Gaze turned to ask Martha where her mother was but, even before she could say a word, her unspoken question was answered. There, on a large box behind the door, lay Elizabeth Mundell, still in her nightclothes, with a cord tied tightly around her throat.

Ann called out for assistance and a number of people from other rooms inside the house, came to her aid. A baker's boy actually cut the cord around Elizabeth's neck whilst Ann ran to fetch a surgeon. It was all to no avail. Elizabeth Mundell was dead.

The inquest on Elizabeth opened that same day and, after the proceedings had closed, Ann and Martha returned to Providence Place, along with Ann's husband, Edward Gaze, who said that he would lay out Elizabeth's body. In preparation for this sad duty, Edward remade Elizabeth's bed and, as he did this, he found that the mattress was wet. It was not, however, wet on top. It was the underside of the mattress that was damp, suggesting that it had been turned. This too appeared to be somewhat curious. Nevertheless, despite their growing suspicions, Ann and Edward asked Martha Browning if she would like to stay with them, until after the funeral. Martha accepted this kind offer and stayed with the Gaze family on both Monday and Tuesday night.

On Wednesday 3 December, Martha Browning announced that she needed to change a £5 note and went to a local shop to carry out that task. She returned within minutes to say that whoever had given her the note must have played a trick upon her because the shopkeeper had pointed out that it was a prank note. The note looked perfectly real but instead of bearing the legend 'Bank of England', it was headed 'Bank of Elegance'. Ann and Edward now knew for certain that all was not as it should be. They knew that Elizabeth Mundell had owned two such notes and, as if further proof were needed, the note that Martha now held in her hand bore a tell-tale grease spot which Edward had seen before. He was certain that this note must have been taken from his mother-in-law.

On the pretext of reporting this spurious banknote to the police, Edward said that he would gladly accompany Martha to the police station. Martha did not seem particularly keen to speak to the police but eventually agreed that it was the best thing to do. The two of them then left Rochester Street and headed for Scotland Yard. However, Martha dawdled along the streets, walking ever more slowly, encouraged by Edward to keep up. Finally, as they approached the police station itself, Martha seemed to half collapse in a faint, and as Edward went to assist her, she cried out, 'I cannot keep it any longer. I murdered the old woman, and deprived your wife of her mother.'

A constable was summoned and he assisted Edward Gaze in taking Martha to the police station. He, in turn, handed Martha over to his inspector and, later that same day, Martha Browning was charged with the wilful murder of Elizabeth Mundell. Her trial, on that charge, took place on 15 December 1845.

The first witness was Ann Gaze, who said that she had known the prisoner for some six months. After telling the

court of Martha's visit to her house, on the morning of
1 December, Ann gave evidence about the cord she had found
around her mother's neck. The cord had been wrapped around
Elizabeth's throat twice, and was tied tightly at the side.

Mary Cheshire was another lodger at Providence Place and
lived in the room next door to the one Martha shared with
Elizabeth. She testified that she had last seen Elizabeth at
10.30 pm, on Sunday 30 November, at which time she was in
good health and good spirits.

At around 7.00 am the following morning, 1 December,
Mary had been woken by a cry of 'Murder!' The cry appeared
to be in Elizabeth's voice and even as Mary rose from her bed,
another cry rang out. This time Mary was certain that it had
been Elizabeth Mundell's voice and she then went next door
to see if she could help in any way. Mary knocked on the
bedroom door but there was no answer. She knocked for a
second time and finally Martha called out, 'Nothing's the
matter.' Mary did not investigate further, but returned instead
to her bed.

Some fifteen minutes later, there was a knock on Mary
Cheshire's door. Climbing out of bed again, Mary found that
it was Martha, who told her that the old lady had been very
poorly. It was Mary who advised Martha to go and tell
Elizabeth's daughter. Martha then left the room, only to
return minutes later with her coat and bonnet on. She said
that she was going to fetch Ann Gaze and asked Mary to keep
an ear open in case Elizabeth made any noise whilst she was
gone.

After Edward Gaze had given his evidence, the prosecution
called Elizabeth Stevens. She had been near Horse Guard's
Parade, on 3 December, when Edward Gaze and Martha
Browning had approached her. By this time, Martha was in a
fainting condition and Edward asked Mrs Stevens if she would
fetch a policeman for him. Mrs Stevens said she was in a hurry
to get to Bayswater but, before she left them, she heard
Martha cry, 'I have done it now. I have done it. For God's sake,
pray for my guilty soul.'

Constable John Adams had been near Scotland Yard, on
3 December, when Edward Gaze had approached him and

told him what had happened and what Martha had admitted. Edward then handed the Bank of Elegance note over to Adams, who then took them both to the police station and handed Martha over to Inspector Partridge.

Mary Fitkin was another lodger at Rochester Street. She testified that on the day of the inquest, she had heard Martha explain that she had been unable to open the bedroom door when Mary Cheshire had knocked because, at the time, she was holding Elizabeth down and washing her face to revive her.

Matthew Little lived at 71 Regent Street, but worked for a master baker close to Rochester Street. He had been at work, on the morning of 1 December, when Martha Browning had rushed in shouting, 'For God's sake, send a man; there is a woman who has hung herself.' Matthew followed her back to the lodgings and it was he who cut the cord from Elizabeth's throat.

The police officer who had taken charge of Martha was Inspector Francis Partridge. When Martha was brought in by Edward Gaze and Constable Adams, she had announced, 'All I can say is, I am an unfortunate creature. You may do with me what you wish.' Later that same day, Inspector Partridge had searched the bedroom where the body lay. In one corner, he found a box which contained a bible. That book bore the name of Martha Browning on the inside front cover, showing that the contents of the box belonged to the prisoner. Inside that same box, the inspector also found a length of cord identical to that cut from Elizabeth Mundell's throat.

The next witness was Mr Charles St Clare Bedford, the coroner who had presided over the inquest on 1 December. Those proceedings had taken place at the *Coach and Horses Inn* and Martha Browning had been the first witness. The statement she had made was then read out in court. It began, 'I have known the deceased, Elizabeth Mundell, for six months, and have been lodging with her there three weeks tomorrow; she, was the widow of Thomas Mundell.'

'She went to bed at eleven o'clock last night. She was quite well then, and was quite sober. She appeared to go to sleep soon, but she awoke me about an hour after we had gone to bed; she was turning about, and was restless. She did not then speak to me; she awoke me again, about four o'clock in the morning, with a sort of plunge in the bed; it quite shook the room.'

'I asked her what was the matter; she said, "Nothing but a dream." I asked her if I should get her anything; she said she did not want anything.'

'She awoke at seven o'clock this morning; she seemed to have a fit; she threw her hands up to her face, and screamed. She screamed, "Murder!" What are you doing to me?'

'I got up and washed her face with water, and asked if I should go for her daughter. I then went to the woman in the next room, and asked her if I had not better go for her daughter. I then went back to deceased's room, and put my bonnet and cloak on; she was then in bed, lying quite quietly. I went to deceased's daughter. I came back with the daughter in about a quarter of an hour. When we returned to the deceased's room her daughter went in first, and I followed her. Deceased was then lying on the box; she had only her night clothes on. A cord was round her neck. I tried to undo the knot; her daughter tried also. I ran out of the house, and went to the baker's shop; the baker came and cut the rope.'

After this statement had been read, the final witness, Dr John Charles Atkinson, was called. He said that he had found Elizabeth's face to be pale, swollen and livid. Her eyes were wide open and blood had issued from her ears and nose. There was also some frothy matter, which had come out of her mouth. The cause of death was either hanging or strangulation, most probably the latter.

With all that evidence, and her statements, at the time of her arrest, there was little doubt as to the final verdict. Martha was found guilty of murder and sentenced to death. There was to be no reprieve and, on 5 January 1846, twenty-three-year-old Martha Browning was hanged outside Newgate prison.

# CHAPTER 14

# Maria Manning
## 1849

Maria de Roux was born in Lucerne, Switzerland, in 1821. Her native tongue was French, but she had received a good education and also learned to speak fluent English. In due course, she emigrated to England and, in 1846, managed to obtain employment as a maid to Lady Blantyre, the daughter of the Duchess of Sutherland. Maria was now moving in much more exalted circles and, on one occasion, even met Queen Victoria.

That same year, 1846, when Maria was twenty-five years old, she travelled with her employer to Boulogne. It was there that she met Patrick O'Connor, an Irishman with a fondness for drink, who was, at fifty, exactly twice Maria's age. Patrick O'Connor worked as a customs officer on the docks in London, but also made a great deal of extra income by lending money at rather exorbitant rates of interest. As a result of this, not only did he have rather a lot of money, but he also held a large amount of shares in railway companies.

In fact, there was another man in Maria de Roux's life, and he too had a connection with the railways. At twenty-seven, Frederick George Manning was much closer to Maria's own age but he had been employed as a lowly guard on the Great Western Railway, a job which he had lost when he was suspected of having been involved in a number of robberies. After this, Frederick had worked as a publican but had also lost that position, due to discrepancies in the accounts.

Both Frederick and Patrick paid court to Maria and each man asked her to marry him. Maria had a difficult decision to make. True, Patrick was a wealthy man who could provide her with all the luxury she desired, but he was a drunkard and much older. Finally, Maria's mind was made up when Frederick told her that he would, in time, come into a large inheritance of his own. So it was that, on 27 May 1847, Maria married Frederick at St James' church in Piccadilly. From that day on, she would be known as Maria Manning, and the newlyweds moved into 3 Miniver Place, Bermondsey.

In due course, Maria discovered that Frederick had lied to her and there was no inheritance in his future. Still, she was by far the more dominant partner in their marriage, and she now decided that she could have the best of both worlds. She remained married to Frederick, but continued to see Patrick and, indeed, often invited him to join her and Frederick for dinner. Maria and Patrick were almost certainly lovers; she supplying him with sexual favours in return for his patronage.

On 23 July 1849, Frederick Manning called at a builder's premises, at 4 Russell Street. There he spoke to Mary Wells and asked her if he might buy 6d worth of lime, saying that he wished to use it to kill an infestation of slugs in his garden. The purchase was agreed and Frederick asked that it be sent around to his house, writing directions down on a piece of scrap paper. Two days later, on 25 July, Richard Welsh, who worked for Mary and her father, duly delivered the lime to Miniver Place. He was asked to deposit the lime into a basket in the kitchen.

On 25 July, the same day that the lime was delivered to Miniver Place, Frederick was making another purchase. On that date he entered Mr Evans' ironmonger's shop in King William Street, where he ordered a specially made crowbar. He was served by William Danby, who said he would deliver it in a few days time. The crowbar was delivered three days later, on 28 July.

Just over a week later, on Wednesday 8 August, Maria Manning was making a purchase of her own. Going into another ironmonger's shop, on Tooley Street, she spoke to an assistant named William Cahill and said she wished to purchase a shovel. She specifically asked for a short-handled one, and finally chose one priced at fifteen pence. The shovel was delivered to Miniver Place, by Cahill himself, at around 7.00 pm.

That same day, Patrick O'Connor was invited to dine at the Mannings' house. When he did call, however, he brought a friend, Mr Pierce Walsh, with him. The friend was made welcome, but at some time during that evening, Maria took Patrick to one side and asked him if he would like to call again the following night, adding that he might come alone so that they could be more intimate. Patrick took the rather obvious meaning, and agreed to return, alone, the next night. However, sometime on that date, Thursday 9 August 1849, Patrick O'Connor vanished.

On the evening of Sunday 12 August, two gentlemen called on the Mannings at Miniver Place. The door was opened by Maria Manning and the two gentlemen identified themselves as Mr William Patrick Keating and Mr David Graham. They explained that they were friends of Partick O'Connor, and indeed worked with him in the Customs House at the docks. They asked, politely, if the Mannings had seen anything of Patrick O'Connor since 9 August.

Maria seemed to be the one who took the lead in answering the question. She confirmed that Patrick had enjoyed dinner with them on 8 August and had been invited to return the following night, but had not attended, nor had he bothered to let them know he was not coming. She also confirmed that she had visited Patrick's lodgings at 21 Greenwood Street, Mile End, but had found that he was not at home.

For the time being at least, Keating and Graham accepted that story.

Unbeknown to the Mannings, another man had also called at their house, looking for O'Connor, on Sunday 12 August. William Flynn was another customs officer and he too had become worried when O'Connor did not turn up for work. Flynn had been to O'Connor's lodgings and discovered that he had not returned home on the evening of 9 August, though an attractive woman had called, twice. Flynn discovered that this woman was Maria Manning, and that O'Connor had arranged to dine with her on 9 August. Calling at Miniver Place on 12 August, Flynn had found no-one home.

Far from satisfied, Flynn then took his suspicions to the police and the next day, Monday 13 August, Flynn returned to Miniver Place but this time he took a plain-clothed policeman, Henry Barnes, with him. Once again, it was Maria who opened the door. Flynn asked if he might speak to Mr Manning but was told that he was not at home. Flynn then stated that he was a personal friend of Patrick O'Connor's, whereupon he and Barnes were invited in and seated in the front parlour.

Questioned further about O'Connor's disappearance, Maria claimed, yet again, that she had not seen him since the evening of 8 August. She confirmed that she had been to O'Connor's lodgings on the evening of 9 August, and again on 10 August, looking for him. Once again, for the time being, things were left at that.

The following day, Tuesday 14 August, Constable James Burton, accompanied by William Patrick Keating, Henry Barnes, and Mr Mead, another friend of O'Connor's, returned to 3 Miniver Place. There was no reply to their knocking but by going around to the back of the house, an entry was forced. Not only was there no sign of the Mannings, but it appeared that they had moved out altogether.

The police investigation continued and, on Friday 17 August, Constable Burton and Constable Barnes were back at Miniver Place to search the premises and determine if any trace of where the Mannings had gone, could be found. It was whilst they were in the kitchen that Barnes noticed that some of the mortar between a couple of the flagstones was still wet. The mortar was scrapped away and one of the flagstones lifted. Immediately, a human toe was revealed and, when the soil was dug away, the rest of a body was discovered. Patrick O'Connor had been found and, from the wounds upon his head, it was clear that he had been the victim of a murder.

It was reasonable to assume that the Mannings had been responsible for Patrick O'Connor's death and, since he was a wealthy man, also reasonable to assume that the motive might have been one of financial gain. The first port of call for the police was to talk to the neighbours. One of these, Mary Ann Schofield, who lived at 12 New Weston Street, told officers that she had a clear view of 3 Miniver Place from her house. She went on to say that, at around 3.15pm, on Monday 13 August, she had seen Maria Manning leaving in a cab. Later that day, at about 5.30 pm, Frederick Manning returned home, knocked on the front door, but there was no reply. Eventually, Frederick was seen going into the house next door, number 2.

The police now began to trace cabmen who may have taken either Maria or Frederick from Miniver Place. They soon traced William Kirk who said that, on 13 August, Maria Manning had approached him whilst he was waiting on the cab-stand. He took her back to 3 Miniver Place and then assisted her in bringing out two large trunks. From there, he drove her to a local stationer's shop, where she bought some luggage cards. Then they travelled on to London Bridge station where Maria left the trunks and then drove on to Euston, where Maria paid the fare and left.

William Byford was another cab driver and he told officers that two days after this, on 15 August, he picked up a male passenger from Bermondsey Square. The man fitted the description of Frederick Manning and Byford had taken him to Waterloo Station. It was then around 8.00 pm and the man said, during the journey, that he needed to catch the 8.30 pm train.

The two trunks which Maria Manning had left at London Bridge station were soon traced, and taken to the police station. They were opened by Superintendent John Haynes, who found a number of items of female clothing, some of which appeared to be heavily bloodstained.

The investigation thus far seemed to indicate that the Mannings had fled London on different days, and in different directions. Maria, it appeared, had headed north, on 13 August, whilst Frederick had travelled south, two days later. Details of both suspects were now telegraphed to police forces throughout the country, as were details of the various share certificates Patrick O'Connor had been known to possess and which were now, apparently, missing from his lodgings.

In fact, one of the two fugitives was already in police custody. Maria Manning, using the surname Smith, had travelled up to Edinburgh where she had tried to sell a share certificate to a stockbroker. Having already been informed that some railway scrip had been stolen in London, they had grown suspicious of the woman with the French accent, and contacted the police. Mrs Smith had been taken into custody and was now interviewed and questioned as to whether she was really Mrs Manning. Eventually, her true identity was revealed and Maria Manning was taken back to London and lodged in Horsemonger Lane Gaol.

Frederick Manning was, however, still at large. Details of the murder of Patrick O'Connor were widely reported in all the national newspapers and one such article was read by a gentleman staying at a hotel in Jersey. By coincidence, he was an acquaintance of Frederick Manning and, upon his return to London, that gentleman told the police that the man they wanted was now staying at a hotel in St Laurence. As a result of that information, Frederick Manning was arrested on 31 August. He too was sent back to London and the confines of the prison at Horsemonger Lane.

In mid-October, the Mannings were moved to Newgate prison, to await their forthcoming trial at the Old Bailey. That trial opened, on Thursday 25 October, before Lord Chief Justice Cresswell. The proceedings lasted for two days.

One of the first witnesses was Constable Henry Barnes, the officer who had found the body on 17 August. He began by stating that he had first noticed the damp plaster between two flagstones. Assisted by Constable Burton, Barnes lifted one of the flagstones and began to dig into the earth beneath. After a few inches, he found a human toe. Digging further, he came upon the loins of a man and, eventually, an entire corpse was revealed. The man, later identified as Patrick O'Connor, was entirely naked. He lay face down in the earth but his legs had been bent back and tied around the haunches with strong cord. The body had been buried in quick lime, no doubt to aid decomposition.

Although the body was almost certainly that of Patrick O'Connor, a formal identification needed to be made. The head had been badly pulped so no facial recognition could be made. In order to affect an identification, the police removed a set of false teeth from the dead man. These teeth were then shown to William Comley, a dentist from Osborne Street, Whitechapel, who confirmed that they were a set he had made for Mr O'Connor.

The body had been examined, in situ, by Dr Samuel Meggitt Lockwood. He found a small, hard protuberance over the right eye and subsequent investigation showed this to be a bullet. Examining the back of the head, Dr Lockwood found extensive fracturing and sixteen separate pieces of bone were removed from the skull. The wounds to the head could well have been produced by a crowbar found inside the house. In Dr Lockwood's opinion, though the wound from the bullet would have eventually caused death, it was more likely that Mr O'Connor had been shot in the head and then finished off by repeated blows from the crowbar.

Ann Harmes lived at 21 Grenwood Street, Mile End, and she testified that Patrick O'Connor had lodged at her house for almost five years. She remembered seeing him leave, early on the evening of 9 August. Some time later, at approximately 5.45 pm, Maria Manning came to the house. She had been there many times before, so she was allowed to go up to Mr O'Connor's rooms without argument. She stayed there, alone, until 7.15 pm. The following day, 10 August, Maria returned at 5.45 pm and again left at 7.15 pm. This testimony was confirmed by Emily Harmes, Ann's sister, who lived with her in Greenwood Street.

William Massey was a medical student and he had lodged with the Mannings, in Miniver Place, until 28 July 1849. He reported various conversation with Frederick Manning which seemed to indicate that the murder of Patrick O'Connor was a premeditated act. Frederick had told Massey that he believed O'Connor to be worth at least £20,000 and spoke of trying to defraud him out of a considerable sum. He asked Massey if chloroform or laudanum could be used to render someone insensitive, so that they might be made to sign a promissory note. Frederick also asked where the most vital part of the head was and also if he knew whether a gun might make a great deal of noise if fired in a confined space.

Charles Bainbridge was a furniture dealer operating from premises at 14 Bermondsey Square. He told the court that the Mannings had contacted him as early as 20 July, seeking to sell all their furniture. A sum was agreed and the transaction

finally completed on 14 August. On that same date, Frederick
Manning asked Bainbridge if he might put him up once the
house at Miniver Place had been emptied. He agreed to pay
10s per week and asked to stay for a fortnight but, after a
couple of days, he left, saying he was going to the country for
a couple of months.

The next witness was Superintendent Richard John Moxey
of the Edinburgh police. He had arrested Maria Manning
when she tried to sell some railway stock in Leith. At first, she
persisted in saying that her surname was Smith but when
Moxey searched her baggage, he found a bill with the name of
FG Manning upon it. She was then taken into custody and
later, after the London police had contacting him, Moxey
charged her with murder. Later still, a trunk in Maria's
lodgings was opened and a large number of share certificates
were found there. The police also found 73 sovereigns, a £50
Bank of England note numbered 11037, six £10 notes and a
£5 note.

Sergeant Edward Langley told the court that, acting on
information received, he travelled to Jersey to arrest the male
prisoner, Frederick Manning. On 27 August, Langley entered
Prospect House where he found Frederick in bed. After
Langley had identified himself as a police officer, Frederick
immediately asked, 'Is the wretch taken?' He went on to say
that if his wife had been arrested, she must have had a good
deal of cash upon her, suggesting that it might be as much as
£1,400. Told that he was being arrested for murder, Frederick
went on to say, 'I am perfectly innocent. She shot him. She
invited him to dinner. The cloth was laid when he came in. She
asked him to go downstairs to wash his hands, and when at the
bottom of the stairs she put one hand on his shoulder and shot
him at the back of the head with the other.'

Evidence was then given on the disposal of one of Patrick
O'Connor's share certificates. On 11 August, Frederick
Manning, purporting to be O'Connor, had gone to the offices
of Killick and Company, share dealers. There he handed a
certificate for twenty £20 shares in the Eastern Counties
Railway Company to one of the clerks, Richard Hammond.
The shares were handed over as security, with Manning asking

for the sum of £110. The money was then handed over to Manning and consisted of a £100 Bank of England note, numbered 15043, a £5 note, and five sovereigns.

Archibald Griffiths was a clerk at the Bank of England. He testified that, on 11 August, the £100 note, numbered 15043 was cashed by a gentleman who signed it on the back, 'Frederick Manning, 7 New Weston Street, Bermondsey.' In exchange he was given fifty sovereigns and five £10 notes. Griffiths was able to confirm that the male prisoner in the dock was the man who had cashed the note.

Having listened to all the evidence, the jury took just forty-five minutes to decide that both prisoners were guilty of murder. Frederick Manning took the verdict quietly but his wife screamed abuse at the judge and jury, shouting, 'You have treated me like a wild beast of the forest.'

The two prisoners were transferred back to Horsemonger Lane gaol to await execution. In the weeks remaining to them, Maria persisted in maintaining that she was innocent of any involvement in the murder but Frederick made a full confession. In that he repeated his claim that Maria had shot Patrick in the head whilst he was standing at the sink. The shot did not kill Patrick, so Frederick then finished him off by raining blows down upon his head with the crowbar. They then both helped to bury him in the makeshift grave.

Maria and Frederick Manning were hanged together, at Horsemonger Lane, on Tuesday 13 November 1849, by William Calcraft. It is said that the largest ever crowd for an execution assembled to watch the event; a crowd estimated at between 20,000 and 30,000, one of whom was the famous author, Charles Dickens. Later, Dickens would write a letter to *The Times* saying how appalling the spectacle was, and castigating the crowd for their boorish behavior.

The execution had one rather unexpected lasting effect. On the morning that she died at the end of the rope, Maria Manning wore a fashionable dress of black satin. So unpopular was Maria that for some thirty years afterwards, genteel ladies refused to be seen in black satin.

# CHAPTER 15

# Ann Merritt
# 1850

James Merritt lived with his wife, Ann, in Pear Tree Place, Clapton, and worked for the East London Waterworks Company. The couple had been married for some seven years and a number of children had been born to the union. Unfortunately, two of those children had died, but the couple still had a son, also named James, and a daughter, named Ann after her mother.

On Wednesday 23 January 1850, Samuel Ketheridge, who lived in Cold Bath Lane, Hackney, and who also worked at the waterworks, walked home with James, after their shift had finished. They parted at around 9.15 pm and, at the time, James Merritt was suffering from nothing more than a slight head cold.

At around 8.00 am, the following morning, 24 January, Samuel called for James so that they might walk in to work together. The door was opened by Ann Merritt, who told Samuel that her husband was in the yard, being sick. James came in a few moments later saying that he had had a basin of broth for his breakfast and a nice hot cup of tea, but perhaps it had turned in his stomach and made him vomit. Still, he seemed to be rather better now and the two men then left for work, together.

By the time the two men reached Clapton Square, James was again feeling rather ill. He also said that a great thirst had suddenly come upon him. So bad was he that the two friends had to call into a nearby public house where James had 2d worth of rum and a little warm water and sugar.

At 11.15 am, Samuel called again at the Merritt's house, where James had returned for lunch. To his surprise, Samuel found James eating nothing more than a bowl of oatmeal gruel, which he was unable to finish. Ann Merritt said she would keep it warm on the stove, but James seemed unimpressed, replying, 'I don't care what you do with it.' James and Samuel then returned to the waterworks together but, by 1.15 pm, James was so ill that he told his friend he would have to go home.

Some time between 5.00 pm and 6.00 pm that evening, Samuel Ketheridge called again at James' house, to drop off the tools he had left at work. Once again the door was opened by Ann Merritt, who told Samuel that her husband was upstairs in bed, and wished to see him. Once in the bedroom, Samuel saw that James was worse than ever and was now complaining of cramp in his feet and legs.

Later still that same evening, Thursday 24 January, at around 8.30 pm, Ann Merritt knocked on the door of the house next door, one occupied by Mary Gillett and her husband. A rather hysterical Ann explained that James was now very ill indeed. Mary and her husband then followed Ann back into her own house and saw James in his bed. He was retching violently and said that he had a burning pain in his chest and a violent pain in his stomach. As Mary Gillett gave James some water, her husband dashed off to fetch the doctor. A doctor did indeed attend and medicine was prescribed but it was all to no avail. At around 12.30 am, on Friday 25 January, James Merritt died.

The inquest opened on Monday 28 January and immediately the authorities ordered that a post-mortem should be carried out. This was performed by Dr Francis Toulmin, who was assisted by Dr Hacon and Dr Welch. Various internal organs were removed and sent for analysis. Those organs were examined by Dr Henry Letheby, who found arsenic in the stomach and liver. As a result, Ann Merritt was arrested and charged with her husband's murder.

Ann faced her trial at the Old Bailey, on 4 March 1850. The first witness was Samuel Ketheridge who detailed the sickness James had complained of, on 23 and 24 January. He was followed to the witness stand by Thomas Denman, a plumber of Clapton Road, who said that he had seen James on Stamford Hill, on 24 January. He was vomiting violently and

Thomas took him into a public house and gave him a small brandy.

James Ashby was another of James' workmates at the waterworks. He had heard that James was ill and went to visit him at 10.40 am on 24 January. It was Ann who answered his knock and told him that James was in the yard, being sick. When James came into the kitchen, Ashby could see that he looked very ill. Ann had made her husband some beef and potatoes for his lunch, but he didn't seem to want it. She then invited Ashby to eat the food, as she didn't want it to go to waste. Ann then told her husband that he might be better off with some oatmeal gruel, which she then started to prepare for him.

Mary Gillett, the neighbour, was the next witness. In addition to detailing Ann Merritt calling at her house and asking her to come in and help with James, Mary was also able to say that she had been passing the house at 1.30 pm, on 24 January. The door was open and Mary looked in and saw that Ann was mixing some oatmeal into a bowl. Mary asked her what she was doing and Ann had replied, 'I am thinning this gruel for Merritt to drink. He is very thirsty.'

On the following Monday, 28 January, just before the inquest opened, Mary had been talking to Ann and the latter had said, 'You know Mrs Gillett that Annie (her daughter) and me ate the remains of the gruel.' A few days later, once it was known that poison had been found in James' body, Ann had also remarked, 'I am innocent. He was a dear, good husband, and it was not likely that I should do such a thing.'

Doctor Francis Toulmin had been called to the Merritt house at some time between 10.30 and 11.00 pm, on 24 January. He had found James in bed, with acute pains in his stomach and severe cramps in his legs. His pulse was also very weak. Dr Toulmin had returned to his surgery and sent back some medicine, but the following morning, he was informed that James had died.

When he called to view the body, on the morning of Friday 25 January, Dr Toulmin had remarked that a post-mortem would be necessary. Ann Merritt immediately objected. She explained that she herself had no concerns about such an examination but James, when he was alive, had objected to such things and she could not now agree, out of respect for him. Surprisingly, perhaps, Dr Toulmin did not press the point and only carried out the post-mortem when requested to do so by the coroner.

Doctor Henry Letheby had examined the internal organs from the post-mortem, on 29 January. He detected eight and a half grains of white arsenic in the stomach and smaller traces in the liver. In his opinion, it was most likely that the fatal dose had been taken some two to three hours before death, though he was not able to state that as a certain fact.

James Urrey was the secretary of the Clapton Benefit Club. He testified that James Merritt had joined the club on 2 February 1848. According to the rules of the society, had James lived until 2 February 1850, his widow would have been entitled to death benefits of £10. However, since he had actually died on 25 January, she was only entitled to the reduced figure of £7 10s.

Constable Alfred Andrews had called at the Merritt house at 9.30 am, on 25 January. At the time, Ann was talking to her neighbour, Mrs Gillett and at one stage, Andrews heard her remark, 'I don't think there is any necessity for a coroner's jury, as my poor dear husband died a natural death.'

Frederick William Ground was an assistant at his father's chemist shop, in Church Street, Hackney, and Ann Merritt was a regular customer there. On 19 January, she had called at the shop, and asked for 2d worth of arsenic so that she might poison some rats or mice. At first, Frederick did not wish to serve her as his father was not present in the shop but Ann explained that they knew her well and she had bought arsenic before. Finally, Frederick agreed to serve her but, as he was about to measure out 2d worth, Ann said; 'I want it in two separate pennyworths; one for myself and one for my sister who lives at a distance and cannot procure it.' Frederick then measured out two separate 1d worth packets and wrapped them both in a larger packet which he clearly labelled 'Poison'.

Inspector James Coward had called at Ann Merritt's house at 10.30 am, on Saturday 22 February. He asked her if she knew of any arsenic being in the house. Ann replied that she did not. Coward then asked if her husband had used arsenic in his work. Ann said he hadn't. Finally, she was asked if she had recently purchased any arsenic and again she replied in the negative. At that point, Coward invited Frederick Ground into the room and he confirmed the purchase of 2d worth of arsenic. Ann now had nothing to say and was arrested on a charge of murder. Later, at the police station, she remarked that she had combined the two parcels of arsenic into one large one, and thrown away the package marked Poison. Her husband had been fond of taking soda powders for his digestion and it was obvious to her that he had taken the arsenic by accident, mistaking it for one such soda powder.

One of the final witnesses was Constable Richard Clark who had accompanied Inspector Coward to Ann's house. After her arrest, Clark was left alone with her for a short time and heard her say, 'I suppose I shall be hanged.'

The final piece of evidence was the statement Ann Merritt had made in the magistrate's court. In this she had said, 'I have nothing to say, but that I never intended him to take it.'

'When I bought it I did intend it for myself if he came home as he had done for several nights past, for I could not live with him as I had done. He came home very comfortable, and I thought no more of it, until the Sunday following, when I burnt it, as it came into my mind that he might take it instead of the soda.'

'As for my giving him anything, it never entered my head. What I said about hanging, was, if I should be hung that minute, I should be hung innocently of giving him anything to do him any harm.'

In the event, the jury found that Ann was guilty as charged, though they did add a strong recommendation to mercy. There could only be one sentence, however, and Ann was duly condemned to death. In due course, though, the jury's recommendation was implemented and the sentence commuted to one of imprisonment.

# CHAPTER 16

# Catherine Wilson
# 1862

Sarah Carnell was very happy with Catherine Wilson, the woman who had come to live with her family as housekeeper. She was kind, attentive and considerate and so close did the two women become that, in due course, Sarah even altered her will so that Catherine would be the chief beneficiary. Not long after that, Sarah caught a chill and her good friend Catherine said she would look after her.

Catherine duly visited the chemists shop and purchased a tonic which would surely put Sarah back on the road to good health. She then returned to Sarah's house where she poured out a generous measure and offered it to her employer.

Sarah took one sip of the liquid and immediately spat it out. It might be expected that medicine should taste somewhat unpleasant but this liquid also burned Sarah's mouth. Even before she could tell Catherine that there was something wrong, Sarah noticed that some of the foul liquid had landed on the bedclothes, which it now proceeded to eat through. As Sarah looked in horror at the ever widening hole in the material, Catherine fled from the house, never to return.

There was something seriously amiss here and Sarah reported the matter to the authorities. The medicine was sent for testing and when the result came back, it was that the liquid Sarah had been given, contained enough sulphuric acid to kill fifty people.

A description of Catherine Wilson was circulated. As a result, she was arrested within a few days and charged with attempted murder. She duly appeared at the Old Bailey on that charge but her defence team claimed that there was no proof that Catherine had put the acid into the medicine. They argued that it might well have been an error at the pharmacists. The jury gave Catherine the benefit of the doubt and found her not guilty, but the ordeal of Catherine Wilson was far from over.

Whilst Catherine had been in custody, the police had been making enquiries into her past. The more they looked into her history, the more it seemed clear that Catherine was actually a mass murderer who had left a trail of bodies behind her.

Catherine had originally come from Boston in Lincolnshire. There she had been housekeeper to a sea-faring gentleman named Peter Mawer. She had looked after Mawer so well that he too had altered his will in her favour. Soon afterwards, he had died and it was clear that he had been poisoned. Mawer, however, suffered from gout and was in the habit of taking a dangerous drug, colchicum. It was simply assumed that he had taken an accidental overdose.

From there, Catherine had moved to London, with a man named James Dixon, and they had lodged with Mrs Maria Soames, at 27 Alfred Street, Bedford Square, commencing in November 1855. In June the following year, Dixon had died and a few months later, in October, Mrs Soames had died too. From there, Catherine had moved to Brixton where a friend, Mrs Atkinson, had come to stay with her. Catherine was behind with her rent at the time and Mrs Atkinson had money. A few days into her visit, Mrs Atkinson died and a telegram was sent to her husband to inform him of the death and that she had been robbed a few days before.

In all, a total of seven possible murders could be attributed to Catherine Wilson. Evidence was collected whilst she had been held in Newgate prison awaiting trial on the attempted murder charge and so, as Catherine walked from the court a free woman, she was immediately re-arrested on a charge of murder. Since there appeared to be more evidence, and thus a stronger case regarding the murder of Maria Soames, that was the charge which the authorities decided to proceed with.

On 22 September 1862, forty-year-old Catherine stood in the dock at the Old Bailey for a second time. The case for the Crown rested in the hands of Mr Clerk and Mr Beasley, whilst Catherine was defended by Mr Oppenheim, Mr Williams and Mr Warton.

The first witness was Samuel Emery Barnes, the half-brother of Mrs Soames. He lived in Highbury House, Holloway and told the court that he had last seen Maria alive on Friday 17 October 1856.

She had last called at his house on the previous Wednesday, 15 October, at some time between 2.00 pm and 3.00 pm. She had been in perfectly good health and had enjoyed dinner with him. She had asked Samuel for £10 but he only had £9 in gold on his person, so gave her that. Samuel explained that when Maria's father had died he had left her a large sum of money and as executor of the will, he was in charge of that cash. Maria would often call and ask for a sum from that money and indeed, some three or four months ago, Samuel had given Maria £40 from that same legacy.

Referring in detail to Maria's finances, Samuel was sure that she had no financial concerns. She owned two properties in Alfred Street; her own house at number 27 and another at number 13. She let rooms out to lodgers and, in all, had an income of somewhere between £80 and £100 per year; more than enough to live on.

On the Friday after Maria's visit, Samuel received a letter from one of her daughters, saying that Maria was unwell and he should come to see her as soon as possible. He arrived at 27 Alfred Street at about 9.30 pm to find Maria in bed. She complained of sickness and severe pain in her head and body. He stayed there for perhaps a full hour, during which time Maria was attended to by Catherine Wilson.

The next morning, Saturday 18 October, a cab arrived at Samuel's house with a message that his half-sister had died in the early hours. He went back to Alfred Street immediately and viewed her body, noting that her face was very distorted and her hands were clenched. Samuel was far from satisfied as to what might have caused Maria's death and insisted that there should be a full post-mortem and an inquest.

Ann Maria Naack was the next witness. Ann told the court that she was twenty-six years old and the wife of Herman Naack, a watchmaker. She was the eldest daughter of Maria Soames and, in 1856, had lived with her, at Alfred Street. Her younger sister, twenty-four-year-old Sarah, also lived there and the two sisters shared a room together.

Ann recalled Catherine Wilson coming to lodge with them in November 1855. At the time she had a man named James Dixon with her, who Catherine said was her brother. There was also a maidservant named Elizabeth Hill. These three took the first floor, unfurnished and, almost immediately, Catherine became very friendly indeed with Maria.

Referring to Maria's visit to her half-brother, on 15 October 1856, Ann remembered that she returned to the house some time between 4.00 pm and 5.00 pm. Soon after 5.00 pm, Maria, Ann and Sarah all enjoyed afternoon tea together and they were just finishing when Catherine Wilson came into the kitchen and asked Maria if she would go up to her room as she had something she wished to say to her in private.

Maria returned to the kitchen soon afterwards and did not reveal what this private matter might have been.

At 8.00 pm that evening, Ann had gone across to the other house at 13 Alfred Street, so did not see her mother again that evening. She returned to number 27 later and, as usual, slept in the same room as her sister Sarah.

At 6.00am the next morning, Thursday 16 October, Maria had come downstairs at 6.00 am and told Ann and Sarah that she had been very ill during the night. She had had some sort of bilious attack and so bad had this been that she would have to go straight back to bed.

Maria had suffered from bilious attacks in the past, though they were very rare indeed, so Ann thought nothing more of the matter for the time being. Later that morning she had seen her mother in bed and she seemed to be much worse. Luckily, Catherine Wilson was on hand to look after Maria.

Throughout that Thursday and on into the next day, Friday 17 October, Maria grew steadily worse. Dr Whidbone was called in to see Maria and, after examining the patient, returned to his surgery to make up a tonic, which he then had sent round to Alfred Street. Curiously, Ann noticed that it was Catherine who took charge of this tonic and administered it to Maria. Even more curiously, after administering each dose, Catherine took the bottle of medicine away, put it into her own bedroom, and locked the door. When asked to explain this, Catherine had said that the doctor had ordered her to take charge of it.

Ann reported one other curious fact. At one stage, Maria had said that she was feeling much better. Immediately, Catherine had said that this must be down to the medicine and she should have another dose without delay. The medicine was administered and Catherine suddenly had a relapse and began vomiting and retching again.

Maria had died between 3.00 am and 4.00 am on the Saturday. The funeral took place a few days later and after this, Catherine had taken Ann to one side and said that before her death, Maria had borrowed £10 off her. Ann was most surprised that her mother should have done this but Catherine produced a written document, which appeared to be in Maria's handwriting. This money was paid back, partly in cash and partly by allowing Catherine to live rent free for a time. Finally, Ann was able to say that Catherine had remained in Alfred Street for a couple of months after Maria had died.

Ann's sister, Sarah Soames, was the next person to give evidence. She confirmed much of what her sister had said but added that when Catherine had first arrived at the house, she told them that her pocket had been picked and she had lost £70. Strangely, she refused to report this theft to the police.

Sarah was also able to say that during her mother's illness, she had seen Catherine giving Maria some mixture of brandy and egg. Catherine brought this to Maria's bedroom already prepared and gave her several doses each day.

Harriett Jane Stevenson was now living in Pratt Street, Camden Town but at the time of Maria's illness and death, she and her husband Sampson had been living at the house in Alfred Street. Harriett was very heavily pregnant at the time and was due to give birth any day. As this was her first child, Harriett was rather nervous and had asked Maria if she would assist her during her confinement. Maria had agreed.

Early on the morning of Thursday 16 October, Harriett had gone into labour and called Maria down to assist as she had promised. This was at 4.00 am and Maria had come down but said she felt very ill and would be unable to help after all. Even as she spoke, Maria vomited into a pail and only stayed for two or three minutes before going back to bed.

Emma Rowe lodged in the other house at 13 Alfred Street and was a close friend of the family. She confirmed that Maria was well on the Wednesday, but very ill on the Thursday. At one stage during Maria's illness, Emma had been inside Catherine Wilson's room and noticed two medicine bottles on the mantlepiece, both containing a pale yellow liquid. When asked why there was two, Catherine said that the large one was Maria's and the other belonged to her. There was, however, one other crucial piece of information that Emma was able to relate.

Just half an hour after Maria had died, on the Saturday morning, Catherine had asked to speak to Emma in private. They went into Catherine's room again and it was there that Catherine said that this was not a natural death. She went on to relate that Maria had been engaged in a secret liaison with a man who had borrowed money off her. The sum of £80 was mentioned and apparently, this man had lied about his circumstances. Once Maria knew that she had been cheated in this way, she had decided to take her own life. Finally, as if proof were needed, Catherine said that she was sure that a letter would arrive on Monday. This would be from the man and no doubt would be, like all the others, a demand for more money. That letter duly arrived on the Monday and did ask for a further £10.

Eliza Frances Matthews lived in Amwell Street, Pentonville, and had been a friend of Maria Soames for some sixteen years. After Maria's death, she had gone to the house to pay her respects and was shocked to see the distorted face and clenched fists. Catherine Wilson was in the room as Eliza remarked, 'Her's must have been a bad death.'

Catherine had replied, 'Poor dear. Ah you don't know all.' Eliza now pressed her on this point and Catherine informed her that Maria had been about to get married, to a man she had met at Islington. Her daughters and her brother knew nothing of this, as it had been a profound secret. She went on to say that Maria had found out that the man was only trying to get money out of her and once again, Catherine said that there would be a letter on the Monday.

Catherine had also suggested that Maria had taken poison to another of her old friends, Sarah Allen. At the time of the trial, Sarah Allen was suffering from diptheria so her deposition was read out in court. In this she stated that Catherine had said to her:

> *I know all her secrets, and I am the only one who does, but I want to keep it secret for the sake of her daughters. She has taken poison.*

John Henry Baker had travelled from Boston to London, to give his evidence. Although he did not testify on any of the main circumstances surrounding the death of Peter Mawer, he did confirm that he was one of the executors of Mr Mawer's will. Peter had died in October 1854 and his will, leaving his property to Catherine, was dated 15 April 1854. From time to time, he would send money to Catherine, under the terms of the will and sometimes she would write to him. One of those letters was now produced in court and in it, Catherine had misspelled one word. She had written 'Wensday' for Wednesday.

The letter purporting to come from the mysterious man from Islington, had arrived at Alfred Street on the Monday after Maria's death. Mr Baker now examined that letter and said that in his opinion, it was in Catherine's hand but she had disguised it somewhat. This was confirmed by John Softly Sneath, the editor of the *Lincolnshire Herald*. He had known Catherine for some twelve years and agreed that she had disguised her handwriting, but the letter had been written by her.

As if further proof of this were needed, the letter was then read out in court. In part, it read:

> *Send me word if you was not well after you got home on Wensday.*

The spelling of Wednesday, was the same.

Three of the final witnesses were all medical gentlemen. Doctor George Ferris Whidborne, practised from 61 Guildford Street, Russell Square. He had been called to see

Maria, on Friday 17 October, and found her to be very ill. He asked her what she had eaten and she replied that she had had some pork pie. This had been given to her by Catherine Wilson, who then produced the remains of the pie for the doctor to look at. This was unlikely to be the source of the illness, however, as some of the same pie had been eaten by Maria's daughters and by Catherine herself and none of them showed any ill effects.

Dr Whidborne said that he would prepare a mixture of Batley's sedative, a mild preparation of opium, and had this sent round from his surgery. Later that same day, when he discovered that the illness was not improving, he prepared a slightly stronger solution and had that sent round too. The doctor also told the court that he had issued no instructions to Catherine Wilson, to say that she alone should take charge of the medicine.

After Maria had died, Dr Whidborne performed a post-mortem at the request of Samuel Barnes, her half-brother. He had found the mucous membrane of Maria's stomach and bowels were inflamed and gave that as the cause of death. He had tested the stomach contents for the usual metallic poisons such as arsenic, mercury and antimony, and found none. However, Dr Whidborne had been called to Alfred Street earlier in the year when James Dixon had died and at that time he discovered that there was colchicum in the house. There was no known test for that poison, but the symptoms it would have produced were identical to those displayed by Maria Soames.

Once Catherine had been arrested and charged with murder, Maria's body was exhumed. Samples of various organs were taken and these were sent to Dr Alfred Swains Taylor of Guy's Hospital. Dr Taylor had made a thirty-year study of poisons and he had tested the organs, on 29 July 1862. He had found no trace of any detectable poison, but agreed that the symptoms shown by Maria were consistent with colchicum poisoning. This evidence was confirmed by the third medical witness, Dr Thomas Nunnelly, who was a Fellow of the Royal College of Surgeons.

The jury, having listened to all the evidence, took almost

St Margaret's Church. It was here that the head of John Hayes was placed on display. *Author's collection*

The Tyburn gallows, where Catherine Conway, Elizabeth Banks and Margaret Harvey were hanged in 1750. *Author's collection*

Elizabeth Brownrigg,
who cruelly murdered
her servant girl.
*Author's collection*

An engraving of the
time, showing how the
Brownrigg crime was
committed.
*Author's collection*

A contemporary illustration of Newgate prison, where Elizabeth Taylor was hanged. *Author's collection*

One of the share certificates stolen by the Mannings. *The National Archives*

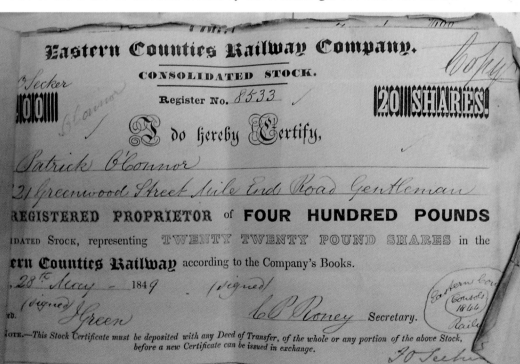

Maria Manning, who plotted a murder for gain. *Author's collection*

A note from the authorities stating that the death sentence on Maria Manning was 'just'. *The National Archives*

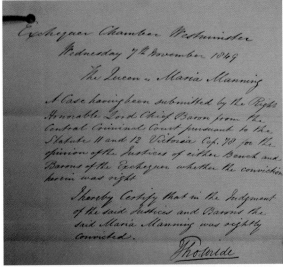

Horsemonger Lane prison, an illustration of how miscreants were hanged on the roof. *Author's collection*

Florence Bravo. Did she poison her husband as some believed? *Author's collection*

Charles Bravo, who died from antimony posioning. *Author's collection*

The Priory, in Balham, where Charles Bravo met his death. *Author's collection*

Treasury
4 Aug. 1876

Sir,

I beg to call your attention to the
fact that the Inquest on the late Mr
Bravo (in which the Jury has agreed
to continue to sit) and certain local
races will probably attract a large
concourse of people to this neighbourhood
on Monday next being a Bank Holiday.

Many of these people will no doubt
turn their attention from curiosity
to Mrs Bravos house known as "The Priory"
and it seems desirable that steps should
be taken to place sufficient Police
Force on the day in question in the
neighbourhood of that house to prevent
the intrusion of the public on the premises
and to guard against any damage
being done to the house or

to

A contemporary letter from the Treasury, pointing out that crowd control might be a problem at the Bravo inquest. *The National Archives*

# CERTIFICATE OF SURGEON.

### 31 Vict., Cap. 24.

I, *Philip Francis Gilbert* the Surgeon of Her

Majesty's Prison of *Newgate* hereby

certify that I this Day examined the Body of

*Mary Eleanor Pearcey* on whom Judgment of

Death was this Day executed in the said Prison;

and that on that Examination I found that the

said *Mary Eleanor Pearcey* was dead.

Dated this *23rd* Day of *December 1890.*

(*Signature*) *P. F. Gilbert*

Confirmation that Mary Eleanor Pearcey had been executed. *The National Archives*

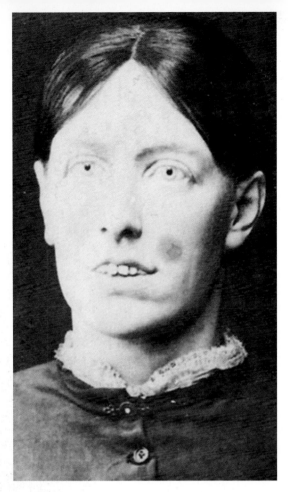

Mary Eleanor Pearcey. This waxwork of her appeared in Madame Tussauds for many years after her death. *Author's collection*

Newgate prison, where Mary Eleanor Pearcey was hanged. *Author's collection*

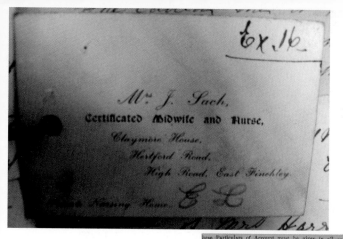

Amelia Sach's
business card.
*The National Archives*

Amelia Sach's Post
Office account book.
*The National Archives*

The receipt to Ada Galley,
signed by Mrs Sach.
*The National Archives*

Another receipt signed by Amelia Sach
and produced as evidence at her trial.
*The National Archives*

Mr Justice Darling, who sentenced
Sach and Walters to death.
*Author's collection*

The Old Bailey, where Clara Alice White
faced her trial for murder. *Author's collection*

Marie Fahmy – a picture
taken before her marriage.
*The National Archives*

Another picture of Marie Fahamy, this time
wearing the veil her husband demanded she
wore in public. *The National Archives*

Hella Christofi, the murdered
woman. *Author's collection*

Styllou Christofi, the Cypriot
accused of the brutal murder of her
daughter-in-law. *Author's collection*

The room where the original Christofi attack took place.
*The National Archives*

The garden fork used to secure the door to the yard at the Christofi murder house.
*The National Archives*

Another view of the room where Hella was attacked. Her blood was found on the iron tray at the foot of the stove.
*The National Archives*

The rear wall at the Christofi's, which a neighbour looked over to see what he thought was a mannequin on fire.
*The National Archives*

The body of Hella Christofi in situ.
*The National Archives*

The badly burned body of Hella Christofi.
*The National Archives*

David Blakely, the man shot by Ruth Ellis.
*Author's collection*

Ruth Ellis, with Desmond Cussen, the man who always denied providing her with the murder weapon.
*Author's collection*

The *Magdala Tavern*. Notice the bullet holes in the wall. David Blakely died close to the newsagents next door.
*Author's collection*

The car which Blakely drove down to the *Magdale* and which he tried to run around in order to escape his assailant.
*The National Archives*

Another picture of David Blakely.
*Author's collection*

David Blakely in the mortuary. *The National Archives*

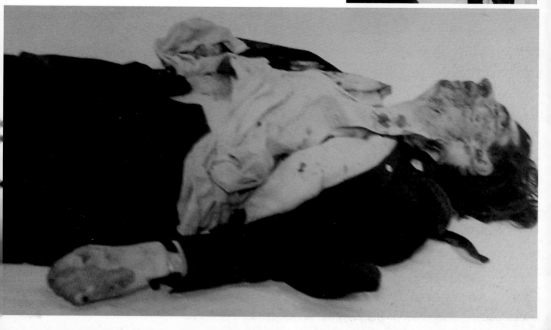

HOME OFFICE,

WHITEHALL.

11th July, 1955

Sir,

    I am directed by the Secretary of State to inform you that,
having given careful consideration to the case of Ruth Ellis, now
lying under sentence of death in Holloway Prison, he has failed
to discover any sufficient ground to justify him in advising
Her Majesty to interfere with the due course of law.

    I am, Sir,

      Your obedient Servant,

*F. a Newsam*

Director of Public Prosecutions,
12, Buckingham Gate,
    S.W.1.

Confirmation
from the Home
Office that the
Ruth Ellis death
sentence would
be carried out.
*The National
Archives*

The end of Ruth Ellis' confession, signed by her. *The National Archives*

three hours to decide that Catherine was guilty as charged and she was then sentenced to death by Mr Justice Byles.

At 8.00 am, on 20 October 1862, Catherine Wilson was hanged outside the debtors' door of Newgate prison, by William Calcraft as a crowd estimated at 20,000 looked on.

Though she could not know it, Catherine would be the last woman ever executed in public, in London. Only four more women ever suffered the ignominy of a public hanging. On 28 December 1863, Alice Holt was hanged in public, in Chester. Three years later, on 3 March 1866, Mary Ann Ashford was hanged at Exeter. Ann Lawrence was hanged at Maidstone, on 10 January 1867 and on 2 April 1868, Frances Kidder became the last woman ever to be executed in public when she was hanged, also at Maidstone. Later that same year, on 28 December, Priscilla Biggadyke became the first woman ever to be executed within the privacy of the prison, when she was hanged at Lincoln.

# CHAPTER 17

# Florence Bravo
# 1876

Florence Campbell was born in 1845, the second child of a family of seven. Florence had quite a privileged childhood; her father, Robert, had made a substantial fortune in Australia and when the family returned to England, he was able to purchase a country residence in Berkshire and a house in Lowndes Square, Knightsbridge.

In 1864, when Florence was just nineteen, a trip to Canada led to a meeting with a dashing Grenadier Guards Captain, Algernon Lewis Ricardo. The two appeared to be besotted with each other and even Florence's father was impressed by Ricardo's background. His father was a Liberal MP and his mother, a sister to the Duke of Fife. The liaison was encouraged, with the result that within three months, Florence and Algernon were married. So pleased was Mr Campbell, that he settled an income of £1,000 on his newly married daughter.

There were, however, problems in the new relationship. Ricardo was dedicated to his life in the army, but Florence had no ambitions to be an army wife, possibly involving travel to the far-flung corners of the Empire. After much discussion, she persuaded her husband to leave the army and take a position in London.

Algernon Ricardo did try to make a success of civilian life. At various times he took positions with both his father and Florence's father, but neither worked out. He could not settle into such a sedentary life and took to drink. There were also rumours that he spent much of his free time in the company of other women. What is certain, is that there were many arguments between man and wife.

Things came to a head one Christmas, when Ricardo insulted one of Florence's sisters. Florence remonstrated with him and Ricardo retaliated by striking her in the face three times. A tearful and rather angry Florence left the marital home and returned to her parent's house.

Perhaps Florence expected that her parents would support her in her plans to obtain a legal separation from Ricardo, but they were appalled at the idea. For them, marriage was forever and if she had made a bad match, then she would just have to live with it. They encouraged Florence to return to her husband and sort matters out, but she would have none of it. After a furious argument, a compromise was agreed upon. Florence would take some time to think things over, by taking a brief holiday at the Hydro, a spa in Great Malvern.

The Hydro was chosen because the Campbells knew that it was run by Dr James Manby Gully, an old family friend. Florence had known Dr Gully since she was a child, so who better to offer her friendly advice. Unfortunately for the Campbells, though, Dr Gully agreed with Florence and said he would support her in seeking a legal separation from her alcoholic husband. He even arranged for her to rent a house in Great Malvern and the two spent a good deal of time together. At one stage they even took a holiday together, in Bavaria, and it was there, despite the fact that Dr Gully was much older, the two became lovers.

In April 1871, Algernon Ricardo died from alcohol abuse, in a hotel room in Cologne. Since he had not made a new will after his separation from Florence, all of his estate now became hers. Florence inherited the considerable sum of £40,000. Now she could do whatever she wished. Without delay, Florence moved back to London, buying the Priory, a large house in Bedford Hill, Balham. Dr Gully was persuaded to leave Great Malvern and move down to the capital too. He also bought a house in Balham, some five minutes walk from the Priory.

In addition to buying the house, Florence was now able to take on whatever servants she wished. One of those, Jane Cox, became a very close friend to Florence and soon became more of a personal companion. Florence was now perfectly happy.

She had a fine house, good servants, a close companion in Jane Cox, a lover in Dr Gully, and a place in respectable society. Unfortunately, it was not to last.

On one occasion, Florence and Dr Gully were invited to spend a weekend with her solicitor and his wife, who lived in a large house in Surrey. One afternoon, the family were all out, leaving Florence and Gully alone in their house. When they returned, they found the couple making love on the settee. Shocked and appalled, the solicitor asked Florence and the doctor to leave his house immediately. The matter became common gossip amongst the servants, who passed the details on to other servants and in this way, polite society in general got to hear of the scandal. Eventually, even Florence's parents heard, with the result that they cut off all contact with their daughter. Society in general began to shun both Florence and Dr Gully.

To escape the gossip, Florence and Gully took a holiday in Austria. It was there that Florence found herself pregnant. There was no alternative; Dr Gully had to perform an abortion on her and Florence almost died during the process. From that time on, Florence's relationship with Dr Gully was to be a purely platonic one. The physical side of their relationship was at an end.

Back in London, Jane Cox, the faithful companion, grew ever more concerned about Florence's unhappiness over being ostracised from society. Surely there was a chance that Florence might be forgiven and accepted back into that society, if she was a respectable married woman. With this in mind, Jane engineered a meeting between Florence and an old family friend, Charles Bravo.

Bravo had been born Charles Delauney Turner in 1845, the son of Augustus Charles Turner and his wife, Mary. When Charles was still quite young, his father died and, in due course, his mother married again, this time to one Joseph Bravo. Charles eventually took his step-father's surname, studied law, and became a barrister.

After a few meetings between the two, Florence could see that things were getting serious between her and Charles. Fearful that some of the gossip might reach his ears, she decided to come clean and confess her affair with Dr Gully. To her surprise, Charles took the news well and confessed that he had had his own affair and a child had been born to the union. They agreed to sever all emotional ties with their respective lovers, and concentrate on their new relationship. That relationship developed rapidly and, on 14 December 1875, the couple were married.

What should have been a possibly perfect match, was actually nothing of the kind. Florence was an independent woman with a large fortune. Charles was an old-fashioned type of man who believed that he should rule the household and expected unflinching obedience from his wife. He was furious when Florence refused to settle all her money on him, deciding instead to keep her fortune under the Married Women's Property Act. He was slightly mollified, when she agreed to sign the Priory over to him, in order to keep the peace.

After a honeymoon in Brighton, Charles and Florence Bravo returned to London where she found, to her delight, that Jane Cox had been correct. Society now began to open its doors once again and Florence enjoyed the dinner parties and functions, which she and Charles were now invited to.

Once again, though, what appeared to be the ideal match, was nothing of the kind. Charles had debts of some £400, a large sum at the time, but Florence held a firm grip on the purse strings. In retaliation, he demanded that she fire her personal maid and one of the gardeners, and get rid of all her horses in order to save money. Florence refused and reminded Charles that she ran the household, not him. Many arguments followed and about the only place that Charles could be as dominant as he wished, was in the bedroom. He demanded his conjugal rights and often forced his wife to have sex. There is also the possibility that he forced her into practices she found abhorrent, including sodomy.

It wasn't long before Florence found herself pregnant again but she miscarried after a few weeks. She suggested to Charles that she might like to have a short holiday in Worthing, in order to recuperate, but his reply was to strike her. Another pregnancy soon followed, only to end in another miscarriage.

With each event, Florence's health grew ever weaker and she managed to convince herself that one more pregnancy might kill her.

In April 1876, Charles returned home badly shaken. He had been for a ride but his horse had bolted and it was with some considerable difficulty that Charles got the beast under control again. At the time, Florence was also feeling rather unwell so, for once, there were no arguments, when it was decided that they would sleep in different rooms that night. It was the night of 18 April.

In the early hours of the morning of 19 April, Charles Bravo appeared on the landing, shouting for hot water and his wife. He was attended to by Jane Cox, who roused Florence. She in turn insisted that Charles should drink a mustard emetic and also have a mustard foot-bath. This had little effect and over the next few days, Charles grew sicker. He was attended by a host of doctors, one of whom was the Queen's surgeon, Sir William Gull. All agreed that Charles had taken some sort of irritant poison, but without knowing what that poison was, they were unable to treat him. Asked what, if anything, he had taken, Charles refused to give any details.

The severity of Charles' condition increased and, on 21 April 1876, he died in his bed. A later post-mortem finally revealed the cause of his condition. Charles Bravo had ingested a massive dose of tartar emetic, which contained antimony. The question was, who had administered that poison?

An inquest was opened, during which Jane Cox testified that before his death, Charles had confessed to taking the poison himself. Knowing some of the history of Florence Bravo and keen to avoid a public scandal, the coroner tried to rush through the proceedings and urged the jury to return a verdict that Charles had taken his own life. The jury were having none of it, and returned an open verdict.

That verdict, and the subsequent revelations in the press, led to a public outcry and a demand that the case be reinvestigated. Such was the pressure that, eventually, the Attorney General ordered that a second inquest be held. At that inquest, Jane Cox withdrew her claim that Charles had confessed to her and, in the course of the hearing, all the details of Florence's past were revealed. Her affair with Dr Gully was now public knowledge, plastered over the newspapers of the day. The public revelled in the sordid stories of sex, affairs, miscarriages and possible poisonings.

Doubt, however, still remained and there was still the possibility that Charles had indeed taken his own life. Some people, of course, suspected that Florence had poisoned Charles. Others thought it might have been Jane Cox, who Charles wanted to dismiss. Still others felt that Dr Gully, a medical man with access to antimony, might have killed Charles, in the hope that it might lead Florence back into his bed.

In the event, it was for the jury to decide and, eventually, they returned the verdict that Charles had been murdered but added: '…there is not sufficient proof to affix the guilt upon any person or persons'. Florence Bravo was a free woman, and no charges were ever brought against her, but in the eyes of the press and the public, she had already been found guilty of wilful murder.

This time, Florence Bravo did not regain her position in society. Two years later, in 1878, and at the age of just thirty-three, she drank herself to death in Hampshire. Five years later, in 1883, Dr James Gully, possibly the only man who had ever made Florence truly happy, died in London. He was seventy-five years old.

# Chapter 18

# Caroline Perry
# 1884

Augusta Scott was a very happy woman. Married to Albert, Augusta lived in Uxbridge with her four children, the youngest of whom was Lottie Marian, who by June 1884, was one month short of her second birthday. There was one other occupant of the house: seventeen-year-old Caroline Perry, who had worked for the Scotts, as a domestic servant, for almost three weeks.

On the afternoon of Thursday 19 June, Augusta asked Caroline to put Lottie into her pram, meet the two eldest children as they left school, and post a letter for her along the way. Augusta did not have any stamps to hand, so she also gave Caroline two pence, and told her to call at the post office first, and buy a 2d stamp. It was around 4.00 pm when Caroline left the house, pushing Lottie in her perambulator.

At 5.30 pm, Augusta Scott's two eldest children arrived home from school alone. They explained that they had indeed been met at school, by Caroline, but she had only walked part of the way home with them, before sending them on ahead and going back the way she had come. Augusta thought that the most likely explanation was that Caroline had forgotten about the letter and turned back to purchase the stamp. She would no doubt arrive home in due course.

It was not until one hour later, at 6.30 pm, that William Ginns, a neighbour, turned hurriedly into Augusta's front garden, pushing the perambulator. Augusta looked inside, and found her child, dead, with a scarf tied tightly around its neck. Of Caroline Perry, there was no sign.

A doctor was called, as were the police, and a search organised for Caroline. In the event, the search was unnecessary, for, that same evening, Caroline walked into

Uxbridge police station and gave herself up. Later still, she was formally charged with the murder of Lottie Scott.

Caroline Perry appeared at the Old Bailey, before Mr Justice Hawkins, on 28 July 1884. The case for the Crown was led by Mr Poland, assisted by Mr Montague Williams. Caroline's defence lay in the hands of Mr Purcell.

Augusta Scott detailed the events of 19 June. After Mr Ginns had brought Lottie home, another neighbour, Mrs Burnham, had come to offer what assistance she could. It was Mrs Burnham who managed to untie the scarf from Lottie's neck. Augusta recognised that scarf as one that belonged to Caroline Perry.

Various witnesses were then called, who were able to detail some of Caroline's movements after she had left the Scott's house. Mary Ann Sargood lived in Park Road, almost opposite to Grove Road and, on 19 June, she had been taking advantage of the warm weather and was sitting in her garden, by the gate. She saw Caroline, pushing the pram, at around 5.30 pm. At the time, Caroline was a few yards from Chippendale Alley, heading towards the Scott house. The two eldest Scott children were some yards in front, holding hands and singing. They walked on towards home as Caroline turned on her heel and began pushing the pram back towards the *Eight Bells* public house.

Alfred Bailey was a nine-year-old schoolboy and, on 19 June, he was standing by Chippendale Alley when he saw Caroline at the entrance. She had a pram with her and the baby was crying. Though he could not hear what was said, Alfred saw Caroline speak to the child in a kindly manner. The baby stopped crying and Caroline then walked on towards the *Eight Bells*. At the time, she was reading a book and walking rather slowly.

At about the same time, Hannah White was walking from the direction of the *Eight Bells*, towards Augusta Scott's house. As she passed down Park Road she saw Caroline, who was now standing at the back of the pram. She had a book in her hand but wasn't reading it. Instead, she seemed to be flicking through the pages as if she were searching for a particular part. As Hannah passed the pram, she glanced in and saw that the baby was lying down, with a cotton hat pulled down over its face.

Jane Edith Leman was just thirteen and lived in Pleasant Place, Uxbridge. On 19 June, she was walking up Chippendale Alley. As she turned into Park Road, Jane saw Caroline leaning against a wall. Jane then saw Mary Ann Sargood in her garden and spoke to her briefly. As she did, the two Scott children passed them on their way home.

Later that same afternoon, Jane walked back towards the *Eight Bells* and saw the pram against a hedge. Caroline was nowhere to be seen so, concerned for the baby, Jane went to the pram to see if all was well. The hood of the pram was now up but, looking inside, Jane saw that the baby was lying on its back with its eyes closed. There was a good deal of foam around the child's mouth and Jane believed that it might have had some form of fit. Running for help, Jane found Mr Ginns, who came to her aid.

William Ginns was on his way home from work, when Jane Leman ran up to him and said she was afraid that a baby was ill. William took a look inside the pram and knew immediately that the child was beyond all aid. He then pushed the pram to Augusta Scott's house, a journey that took some eight to ten minutes.

Johanna Lewis Burnham lived three doors down from the Scotts and was in her front garden when William Ginns arrived at Mrs Scott's house. Seeing that she was distressed, Johanna went to see if she could offer any help. Johanna saw Augusta take her daughter from the pram, and noticed that there was a scarf tied tightly around the child's neck. It was Johanna who, with some considerable difficulty, managed to untie the scarf, revealing a deep black mark beneath.

The final witness giving details of Caroline Perry's movements, was Lydia Davis, aged twelve. Her family lived close to Caroline's, so Lydia knew the family well. At some time between 5.00 pm and 6.00 pm, on 19 June, Lydia had been in George Street, Uxbridge when she had seen Caroline running towards her. As Caroline passed, she called out to Lydia, 'Don't say that you have seen me.' She then headed on, towards High Street.

Doctor John Davidson was the medical gentleman called to

Augusta Scott's house. He timed his arrival at 6.30 pm and confirmed that Lottie was dead. Two days later, on 21 June, Dr Davidson performed the post-mortem, which confirmed that the cause of death had been suffocation due to strangulation.

Sergeant Joseph Whitehurst was the officer on duty in Uxbridge police station when Caroline Perry walked in to give herself up. After identifying herself and explaining why she was there, Caroline had handed over to Whitehurst two books: *Uncle Tom's Cabin* and *The Sunday School Hymn Book*. She also gave him the unposted letter given to her by Augusta Scott, and the 2d for the stamp.

Inspector Christopher Blomfield was the final witness. He had been at Uxbridge police station at 11.30 pm, by which time Caroline had been charged and placed in the cells. At one stage he heard a loud, hysterical cry, come from Caroline's cell. Going to check on her, he found her lying on her left side, wringing her hands and crying. Asked what the matter was, Caroline said she had been dreaming of little May.

The last piece of evidence was the brief statement Caroline had made when committed for trial by the magistrates. She had merely said, 'I am not guilty of wilful murder and I reserve my defence.'

No real reason could be given for the death of little Lottie Scott. The jury retired to consider their verdict and when they returned, they announced that they had found Caroline not guilty of murder, but guilty of manslaughter. No evidence had been given to indicate that Caroline was insane, but obviously the jury had thought that this wanton, motiveless crime couldn't have been committed by someone in their right mind.

Spared the death penalty, Caroline Perry was then sentenced to fifteen months' imprisonment, with hard labour.

# CHAPTER 19

# Mary Eleanor Wheeler (Pearcey) 1890

ary Eleanor Pearcey, who preferred to use her middle name, had never actually been married. At one stage she had lived with a man named Pearcey and, even though he had since left her, she continued to use his surname.

Although she could not perhaps be described as the most attractive of women, Eleanor did have a fondness for the company of men and, by 1890, had had a string of affairs. By that same year she occupied three rooms at 2 Priory Street, Kentish Town. Those rooms were paid for by one of Eleanor's admirers, a gentleman named Mr Crichton who lived in Gravesend, but who travelled to London once a week in order to see Eleanor, and take advantage of her sexual services.

Eleanor, however, did not limit those services to just one man. Another of her admirers was Frank Samuel Hogg who lived with his sister, Clara, and their mother, at 141 Prince of Wales Road, also in Kentish Town. Hogg, though, had to be somewhat more circumspect in his visits to Eleanor as he was a married man, with a young daughter, both of whom were named Phoebe, who also both lived at number 141. As for Eleanor, it seemed that Frank Hogg was her favourite lover and, as far as she was concerned, Phoebe Hogg was nothing more than an encumbrance.

On Thursday 23 October 1890, Phoebe Hogg received a hand-written note from Eleanor Pearcey. The note read:

*Dearest, come round this afternoon and bring our little darling. Don't fail.*

The missive was an invitation to come to tea, and to bring baby Phoebe with her.

Phoebe Hogg was unable to go for tea on that particular day and sent a reply to that effect. Eleanor, however, was not to be dissuaded. The following day, William Henry Holmes, a twelve- year-old schoolboy, who lived with his parents at 138 Prince of Wales Road, was sent to the shop by his mother. It was around 11.00 am and as William left the shop, Eleanor Pearcey was waiting outside. She beckoned to William, who went over to see her, whereupon she gave him a penny and a note, asking him to take it to Mrs Hogg at number 141. Eleanor was careful to make sure that William handed the note to Phoebe Hogg herself. This time, Phoebe decided that she would go to tea and left her home, at around 3.30 pm, pushing the baby in a pram.

At 10.00 pm that same evening, Frank Hogg decided to pay a visit to Eleanor and let himself in using a latch-key she had provided him with. Eleanor was not at home and only a single oil lamp burned in one of the rooms. After waiting for some time, Frank hurriedly scribbled a note:

*Twenty past ten. Cannot stay.*

Frank arrived home at Prince of Wales Road some time later but found that Phoebe was not in. Frank assumed that she might have gone to visit her sick father in Rickmansworth, and stayed over for the night.

Frank Hogg rose for work at 6.00 am, on the morning of Saturday 25 October. He returned home at 8.00 am, in order to get some breakfast, and was just being given some food by his sister, when Emma Barraud, the woman who actually owned the house, came in and told them of a dreadful murder. Apparently, the body of a young woman had been found in Crossland Road, close to Swiss Cottage.

Immediately, Clara Hogg dashed out to purchase a morning paper, hoping that it might give more details. There was indeed a story about a horribly mutilated body being found. Having listened to Clara read the story, Frank Hogg decided to go to Rickmansworth to see if Phoebe was with her father after all. Clara, possibly the more practical of the two, decided to call on Eleanor Pearcey.

When Clara Hogg arrived at Eleanor's rooms, she asked if she had seen Phoebe on Friday evening. At first, Eleanor denied seeing her but, questioned again by Clara, she made the curious admission that Phoebe had indeed called on her on the Friday but had asked Eleanor to keep the meeting secret. This was, apparently, because Phoebe had sought to borrow some money. Clara did not believe this for one moment, knowing full well that Phoebe had a terror of being in debt, even for a small sum.

Clara Hogg then announced that she intended to visit the police station at Hampstead, and ask to see the body. Clara asked Eleanor to go with her, more for moral support than anything else, and Eleanor agreed. The two ladies then travelled together to the police station, where Detective Inspector Thomas Bannister listened to Clara's story about Phoebe's disappearance, and then took both women to the mortuary to view the mutilated body.

Immediately, Eleanor said she did not recognise the body and it certainly wasn't Phoebe Hogg. Clara was less certain and pointed out that the body was wearing clothing which was very similar to that which Phoebe possessed. She then asked if the bloodstained face of the corpse might be washed, so that she would have a better idea if this were Phoebe or not.

Once the blood had been washed off the face of the dead woman, Clara had no hesitation in identifying the body as that of Phoebe Hogg. Detective Murray then took them to view a perambulator, which had been found on some waste ground and again Clara made a positive identification.

It was Sergeant Beard, who escorted Clara and Eleanor back to Prince of Wales Road, where both Frank Hogg and his mother, Mrs Styles were questioned. At one stage, the sergeant searched Frank Hogg and found a latch key which didn't belong to that house. Frank soon confirmed that it was the key to Eleanor Pearcey's home, at which point all four were taken to the police station.

The police had little doubt that one of these four had murdered Phoebe Hogg. However, at the mortuary, Eleanor Pearcey had displayed some very curious behaviour. She had been adamant that the body wasn't that of Phoebe Hogg and had tried to physically pull Clara away. Inspector Bannister decided to investigate further and told Eleanor that he would like to inspect her apartments. Eleanor said she had no objections, but asked that she might be allowed to accompany any officers who were sent.

It was around 3.00 pm when Sergeant Nursey and Sergeant Parsons arrived at Priory Street with Eleanor. Having made a quick search of the premises, one of the sergeants went to send a telegram to his headquarters, whilst the other engaged Eleanor Pearcey in conversation. In due course, having received the message, Inspector Bannister arrived and found a number of bloodstains, and possible murder weapons. Asked to account for the stains, Eleanor replied that she had been killing mice. She was then escorted back to the police station, where she was searched by a female officer. Not only did Eleanor have a large number of fresh scratches on her arms and hands, but her underclothes were saturated in blood. She was then charged with murder.

Events moved very quickly indeed. Eleanor Pearcey made just one appearance at the Marylebone police court, on 27 October, when, the evidence having been heard, she was committed for trial. That trial opened on 1 December 1890, before Mr Justice Denman. The case for the prosecution was led by Mr Forrest Fulton, assisted by Mr CF Gill. Eleanor was defended by Mr Arthur Hutton, and the proceedings lasted for four days.

The first witness was John Charles Pearcey. He confirmed that he had known the prisoner for some five years and that he had once lived with her, for a period of three years. He went on to explain that he had left Eleanor, when she had started seeing Frank Hogg. Eleanor had also been seeing other men, and John was not prepared to be just one of her lovers.

Frank Samuel Hogg confirmed that he and Phoebe had married in November 1888, and that his wife had given birth to a baby girl on 11 April 1889, who they had named Phoebe Hanslope Hogg. Turning to Eleanor, Hogg said that he had known her for about four years, and when they first met, she had been living at Bayham Street. He recalled Eleanor moving to Priory Street, in the late autumn of 1888.

Despite his marriage to Phoebe, Hogg had continued to visit Eleanor and she had given him a latch key, some time in December 1889. He admitted that they had been lovers, and the last time they had had sex was on 24 October 1890, the day that his wife and daughter were killed.

Turning to the relationship between his wife and his lover, Hogg then told the court that the two had not been acquainted until Christmas 1889. Eleanor had sent him a note, asking him and his family to spend Christmas Day with her. Hogg had agreed and they spent 25 December and much of 26 December with Eleanor. From that time on, Eleanor used to visit Phoebe at Prince of Wales Road, at one stage even spending a couple of weeks there when Phoebe was ill.

Frank Hogg now turned to the events of Friday 24 October. At the time, his wife's father was gravely ill and not expected to survive. Indeed, he and Phoebe had agreed that if any news came through from Rickmansworth, she was to go to her father's house immediately. For this reason, he was not unduly concerned when he returned home from work and found his wife and child were not there. He then went on to detail the events of the following day, once he had heard about the body of a woman being discovered.

At the end of his testimony, Frank Hogg confirmed that various letters, entered into evidence by the prosecution, were in Eleanor Pearcey's hand, and had been written to him. In one, dated 2 October 1888, she had written:

*My dear F, Do not think of going away, for my heart will break if you do; don't go, dear. I won't ask too much, only to see you for five minutes when you can get away; but if you go quite away, how do you think I can live? I would see you married fifty times over, yes. I could bear that far better than parting with you for ever.*

In another letter, dated 18 November of the same year, Eleanor had written:

*Dearest Frank, I cannot sleep, so am going to write you a long letter. When you read this I hope your head will be much better,*

*dear, I can't bear to see you like you were this evening. Try not to
give way. Try to be brave, dear, for things will come right in the
end. I know things look dark now, but it is always the darkest
hour before the dawn.*

The letter went on to imply that Eleanor would be unable to
live without Frank, and would do anything to keep him in her
life.

The next witness, Clara Hogg, confirmed that she had
known Eleanor Pearcey for about four years, and recalled
Phoebe's illness in February 1890, when Eleanor came to
nurse her. Clara went on to recount the events of the morning
of Saturday 25 October, her visit to Eleanor's home and the
subsequent visits to the police station and the mortuary.

Other people lived in rooms at 2 Priory Street, besides
Eleanor Pearcey. Elizabeth Crowhurst lived there with her son,
William, and she confirmed that she had been away from the
house on 23 October, attending to her sick daughter, who
lived in Great College Street. She did not return home until
around 7.00 pm on 24 October.

William Crowhurst said that he had been at work all day on
24 October. He had left home at 8.30 am and not returned
until 7.45 pm. Approximately forty-five minutes later, he had
occasion to go out into the yard at the back of the house and
noticed some glass on the flagstones. He saw that there were
two broken panes in the kitchen window.

Clara Hogg had testified that Phoebe left home, with the
baby, at 3.00 pm on 24 October. The next witness, Charles
Britt, had a stable in Priory Mews and in order to reach it, had
to pass down Priory Street. He did so at 3.30 pm, on 24
October and saw a woman, with a pram, knocking at the door
of number 2.

Charlotte Piddington lived next door to Eleanor, at number
3, Priory Street. She told the court that she heard the sound
of glass smashing, at some time between 3.00 and 4.00 pm.
Shortly after 4.00 pm she also heard a young child screaming.

Sarah Butler also lived in rooms at 2 Priory Street, with her
husband, Walter. She had been out on 24 October, and
returned home at around 6.00 pm. As she walked down the

passageway, Sarah bumped against a pram. Some ten minutes later, Sarah went back down the hallway and by then, the pram had gone.

Walter Butler had come home a few minutes after his wife and he too bumped into the pram. As he entered, Eleanor Pearcey came out of her rooms and said, 'Mr. Butler, there is a bassinette in the passage, allow me to hand you by.'

From the testimony of these witnesses, the suggestion was that Phoebe had arrived at 2 Priory Street at about 3.30 pm. Within the next half hour, she had been attacked and killed, leaving Eleanor with the problem of disposing of the body. It may be that baby Phoebe was also killed at this time but the next witnesses' testimony would indicate how the bodies were disposed of.

Elizabeth Rogers lived at 7 Priory Street. Elizabeth was walking home on the evening of 24 October and turned into her street at a few minutes after 6.00 pm. As she did, she saw Eleanor pushing a pram before her, walking towards Bonny Street. The pram seemed to be rather awkward to maneuver, and seemed to contain something very heavy. It was covered over with some sort of black material. Eleanor struggled to push the pram up the hill, and Elizabeth last saw her as she turned into Prince of Wales Road.

Anne Gardner had also seen Eleanor pushing the pram, heading into Crossland Road. This was highly significant, for that is where Phoebe Hogg's body was discovered. That discovery was made by the next witness, Somerlea Macdonald, at 7.10 pm. She had seen a woman, lying by the side of the road, with her face covered and Somerlea's first assumption was that the woman was drunk. Some minutes later, Somerlea was making her way back down Crossland Road and noticed that the woman was in exactly the same position. She saw, to her horror, that the woman had been brutally murdered and dashed off towards Swiss Cottage Railway Station, to find a policeman.

The policeman who Somerlea found was Constable Arthur Gardner. He then went to Crossfield Road, where he found Phoebe Hogg, lying on her back, her face covered by a cardigan. There was a great deal of blood on the body and her throat had been cut so deeply that the head was almost severed.

After Gardner had contacted the police station, Inspector Thomas Wright went to Crossland Road to see the body for himself. He reported that:

> *The right leg was perfectly straight, the left leg was drawn under the body, bent up at an angle. The right arm was extended, and the hand clenched. The left arm was drawn up above the shoulder. The face was covered with a brown Cardigan jacket.*

The body of the baby had not been found close to Phoebe's. It appeared that having dumped one body, Eleanor then carried on pushing the pram, with the dead baby still inside it. Elizabeth Andrews lived at 34 Hamilton Terrace, St John's Wood and she told the court that she was leaving her house at 7.30 pm, on 24 October, when she saw a pram parked near the front gate. She returned to her house at 8.40 pm and found that the pram was still there.

Constable John Roser was on his beat and walked down Hamilton Terrace at 10.30 pm. As he passed, Elizabeth Andrews pointed out the pram to him and Roser went to investigate. He removed a rug and found that the interior of the pram was saturated with blood. Roser then took the pram to the police station.

The body of the baby was not discovered until 6.30 am, on 26 October. Oliver Smith was a hawker and he was in Finchley Road, on 26 October, when he noticed something lying in a bed of nettles. Close inspection revealed it to be the body of a child, fully clothed, apart from one missing boot and sock. Smith soon found Constable James Dickerson, and reported the matter to him.

After Sergeant Edward Nursey and Sergeant Edward Parsons had told the court of their visit to 2 Priory Street with Eleanor Pearcey, details were given of the search of Eleanor's rooms. A number of items of clothing had been found, all heavily bloodstained. The were splashes of blood up the walls and there were signs that a rug had recently been scrubbed with paraffin.

Inspector Bannister had also found a bloodstained poker, which had human hairs adhering to it.

Doctor Thomas Bond had examined Phoebe Hogg's body, on the morning of 25 October. He found the bones of the skull were badly fractured. In addition, the throat was deeply cut so that the spinal column was divided, meaning that only the muscles at the back of the neck held the head on. Dr Bond had also examined the hair found on the poker and saw that it was a match to Phoebe's.

The post-mortems on both victims had been performed by Dr Augustus John Pepper. He confirmed that Phoebe Hogg had died from a fractured skull and loss of blood from the throat wound. Turning to baby Phoebe, he had concluded that the cause of death was either smothering or exposure to the cold. He was unable to say if the child had been deliberately smothered or if she might have died when her mother's dead body was dumped onto her in the pram.

After hearing all the evidence, the jury took less than an hour to decide that Eleanor was guilty of murder. She was then sentenced to death. There was no Court of Appeal at this time, but strenuous efforts were made to secure a reprieve. A detailed report, prepared by Dr Forbes Winslow, attempted to suggest that Eleanor had suffered from an epileptic seizure at the time of the attack and was consequently not responsible for her actions. It did nothing to sway the Home Office and, in due course, the death sentence was confirmed.

On Tuesday 23 December 1890, a crowd of some 300 people gathered outside Newgate prison as Eleanor Pearcey was hanged by James Berry. Frank Hogg, the man who she had apparently loved so much, then made a good deal of money by selling the pram and the poker to Madame Tussaud's where they were exhibited for a number of years.

# CHAPTER 20

# Ann Sarah Hibberd
# 1894

I n 1885, Ann Sarah Scotney married William Hibbard. Over the next nine years, the couple had four children, two of whom passed away. By 1894, they lived in two rooms at Ann's mother's house, 77 Cooper Road, off Barking Road, but by now, there was little affection between them.

William Hibbard was a stevedore by trade but much preferred alcohol to work. His usual routine was to work just one or two days each week, keep his family on as little money as possible and spend the rest on drink in one of the local public houses. Once he was in drink, William also mistreated Ann, but he was always very careful not to hit her where bruises might show. Thus, he would strike her on the arms or body and only the family knew the extent of the injuries she suffered.

On Monday 30 July 1894, William came home for his lunch at 12.30 pm. His mother-in-law, Sarah Scotney, was in the kitchen at the time and she saw him go upstairs after he had eaten. Later, he left the house and there was little doubt in Sarah's mind that he was heading for the nearest bar.

At around 2.00 pm, Ann Hibberd took her two children out for a walk. The eldest was able to walk by her side, but she carried the youngest child in her arms. She returned shortly after 3.00 pm, to announce to her mother than 'Mr Bill', the nickname she used for William, was misbehaving with some women in *The Peacock*, a local public house. William had been with Mr Green, the man from next door, and Ann determined to tell his wife what he was up to, but when she went next door, there was no reply to her knocking.

Approximately one hour later, at 4.00 pm, Ann took the children out once again. Sarah Scotney did not see her daughter again that day and the next she heard of her was when a constable knocked at the door, to say that Ann was in custody on a charge of stabbing her husband. The events of the rest of 30 July, were detailed by various witnesses.

Emma Massey was the daughter of the landlord of *The Peacock*, situated in Freemasons Road. Emma worked for her father, as a barmaid, and was on duty throughout 30 July. At approximately 2.00 pm, she had seen two men and two women come into the bar. Though she did not know them at the time, Emma now knew that one of the men was William Hibberd.

Some time later, Ann Hibberd came into the off-sales bar, with her two children. She ordered a quart bottle of gin to take home and a pennyworth of ale to drink on the premises. As the drink was served, Ann asked Emma if her husband was in the other bar. Even before Emma could answer, Ann had looked over the counter, into the other bar, and spotted William, saying, 'Oh, there he is. I can see him.' Ann then asked Emma if William was with any women. Emma, being rather tactful perhaps, said that she didn't know. Ann drank her beer, took the bottle of gin, and left.

William and his friends also left *The Peacock* soon afterwards but, by 5.00 pm, he was back, talking to a group of men around the bar. Some time before 6.00 pm, Ann also returned to the bar, still with her two children. She immediately went up to the group of men and asked William if he would come home. William merely laughed. He then reached into his pocket, produced a penny, and said he would buy Ann a glass of beer. However, once the drink had been served, William picked up the glass and threw it over Ann. He then left the bar, followed soon afterwards by a soaked Ann.

Rather than walk home, William had simply strolled to the next public house, *The Royal Albert*, also on Freemasons Road. William was seen there by Eliza Smith and, a few minutes later, she saw Ann enter the bar, go up to William, and again ask him to come home. Though Eliza did not know the significance of the comment, she heard William laugh and ask Ann if she wanted another glass of ale.

Once again, William walked outside, to be followed by his wife. Eliza Smith left at the same time and Ann spoke to her on the way out, saying, 'My husband is a beast to me. He earned nine shillings on Saturday, and gave me one out of it, but I will do for him with this.' Only now did Eliza see that Ann had taken a knife out of her pocket.

Still not content to return home, William walked back to the first public house, *The Peacock*, where he was seen by Harriett Butcher. Yet again, Ann followed him in and asked him to come home with her. Yet again, William laughed in her face and encouraged everyone in the bar to laugh at her too.

It was not until after 8.00 pm that William finally left the public house, followed again by Ann, who was still carrying one child and dragging the other one alongside her. By 8.15 pm, they were walking down Freemasons Road, and walking towards them was John Barclay and Joseph Storey.

Barclay and Storey were in conversation, and taking little notice of the couple walking towards them. Suddenly, the woman lifted her right hand and appeared to strike the man in the left shoulder. As she did so, she shouted, 'I will kill you; I mean it.'

The man staggered forward, fell to his knees, but then managed to drag himself to his feet. He took some steps away from the woman but she followed him, caught up, and appeared to strike him twice more. Only now did Barclay and Storey see that she held a black-handled knife in her hand. Even as Ann stabbed William, she still held her youngest child in her arms.

Ann Hibberd was soon taken into custody and charged with stabbing her husband. Unfortunately, William did not respond to medical treatment and died from his injuries on Wednesday 1 August. The charge against Ann was then amended to one of wilful murder and she appeared at the Old Bailey, to face that charge, on 10 September 1894. Mr Horace Avory and Mr F Gill appeared for the prosecution whilst Ann was defended by Mr Grantham and Mr Hall.

In addition to the witnesses already mentioned, the prosecution called William Green, the gentleman who had been drinking with William Hibberd on the fateful day. Green stated that he had first met William at around 2.30 pm and they had gone for a drink with two women friends. The two

friends finally parted at 4.30 pm and the next time Green saw
William, he was being taken from the scene of the stabbing, in
a pony and cart. Having heard about the stabbing, Green then
saw Ann Hibberd, with her children, at the corner of Garvery
Road. She seemed to be very emotional and asked Green what
she should do. Green thought it best if the children were taken
home and began to escort Ann there but within moments, they
had been overtaken by a constable, who arrested Ann.

That constable was Francis Kronk who said to Ann, 'You
will have to come along with me, to the station, for stabbing
your husband.' Ann had replied, 'I hope I have killed him. I did
it intentionally.' Later, at the Canning Town police station,
Ann also said, 'I saw him drinking with two women. It was
jealousy.' When she was searched, Ann had a farthing short of
three shillings and five pence on her person.

Constable Henry Taylor had also been close to the scene of
the stabbing, and had gone to offer what aid he could to the
stricken man. It was Taylor who took William Hibberd to the
Seamen's Hospital and helped the medical staff to undress
him.

The doctor who had treated William was Dr Edward
Phillips. He testified that William was brought to the hospital
at 8.55 pm, in a state of collapse. He had a number of wounds,
the most serious of which was one high on the left breast, just
above the heart. Despite prompt treatment, William died at
4.50 pm, on 1 August. Dr Phillips conducted the post-mortem
on 2 August and saw that the stab wound to the chest had
pierced the pericardium and the right ventricle of the heart. In
his opinion, considerable force must have been used in order
to penetrate the clothing.

In the event, having listened to details of the way William
Hibberd had treated his wife, the jury decided that Ann had
received such provocation as would reduce the charge to
manslaughter. They also added a strong recommendation to
mercy. Having avoided the hangman's noose, Ann was then
sentenced to six years' imprisonment.

# CHAPTER 21

# Amelia Sach and Annie Walters
# 1903

I n the year 1902, Ada Charlotte Galley, a domestic servant at Stanley Villa in Finchley, found herself pregnant. Since she had only ever slept with one man, there was no difficulty in determining who the father was but, various circumstances prevented them from getting married. Miss Galley decided that the child, when it was finally born, would have to be taken for adoption.

In August of that same year, Ada Galley saw an advertisement in *Dalton's* newspaper. It read:

*Accouchement before and during. Skilled nursing. Home comforts. Baby can remain. Nurse. Claymore House. Hertford Road, East Finchley.*

For Ada, the most important part of that advertisement was the phrase 'Baby can remain', meaning that Claymore House wasn't merely a safe place that she could go to give birth, but that the baby could remain behind whilst the owners of the house found a suitable home for it. It appeared to be the ideal solution.

Ada wrote to the given address and soon received a reply. In due course, Ada visited the house where she met a woman, who said she was the owner, and gave the name of Amelia Sach. She explained that Miss Galley could come to stay there whenever she wished, at a fee of £1 1s per week. However, during the confinement itself, the fee would rise to £3 3s. Ada Galley said that she found those terms acceptable and moved into Claymore House, on 24 September 1902.

Ada hadn't been at the house for very long when Sach approached her and asked what she intended doing with the child after it was born. Ada explained that her circumstances meant that she would be unable to care for it herself and would welcome Amelia Sach's help with an adoption. Sach explained that she could find a high-class home for the child, where it would be well cared for and loved, but that the fee would be between £25 and £30, a considerable sum of money (c.£1,700 today). Ada said she did not think that she could afford that much, but Sach said she would write to the lady she had in mind to take the child, and see if she would take a lesser amount.

Ada Galley admitted that she was rather confused about this arrangement. Sach had told her that the lady she was going to write to was very wealthy. Ada then said that if she were wealthy, why would she need a sum of money to take the baby? Surely she didn't need the cash. Sach explained that it was the usual arrangement and was to buy clothes and presents for the new baby. Ada said she would write to her baby's father and ask him to pay the money.

On Saturday 15 November, at 8.00 am, Ada Galley was delivered of a healthy baby boy. That same day, she sent a telegram to the father, and at 7.30 pm that evening, he called at Claymore House to see his son. Having done so, he then handed five £5 notes to Amelia Sach, the agreed fee for the forthcoming adoption. As was customary at the time, since banknotes were somewhat rarer in circulation, he had noted the serial numbers 09978 to 09982 inclusive, and that each note was dated 3 September 1902.

Unbeknown to Ada Galley, or the father of her child, a telegram had been sent, by Amelia Sach, on 15 November, the same day the baby was born. The telegram was addressed to 'Walters. 11 Danbury Street, Islington, London'. It was received by the owner of the house, Minnie Spencer, who gave it to her son to pass on to Annie Walters, one of the lodgers.

There had been some very curious occurrences of late at 11 Danbury Street. Mrs Walters had come to lodge there on 29 October 1902, saying that she was a nurse at St Thomas' Hospital. For the first few days, Minnie Spencer's new lodger proved to be little trouble but soon she said that in a few days time, she might well be receiving a baby from a friend of hers, who she named only as Maude. This baby would then be taken to a rich lady in Piccadilly, who would pay her no less than £100. For providing this simple service, Mrs Walters would receive some thirty shillings commission. This seemed rather curious to Mrs Spencer. She knew, of course, that such things went on, but the rich lady and the £100 seemed rather too far fetched to be true.

On Wednesday 12 November, though, a telegram had arrived at the house. Addressed to Mrs Walters, it simply read: 'Tonight at five o'clock'. The sender's address was only given as Claymore House. Mrs Walters left the house almost immediately and did not return until 6.30 pm. When she did, she had a baby with her, a child which she said, was a girl.

From that moment on, Mrs Walter's behaviour became rather strange. She asked Minnie Spencer to go to the shops for her and purchase a bottle and teat, some milk, and, rather strangely, a bottle of Chlorodyne. This was a patent medicine, made from chloroform and morphine, used to aid those who had trouble sleeping. Still, it was nothing to do with Mrs Spencer, who duly purchased the items and handed them over to Mrs Walters.

On the morning of 13 November, Mrs Walters gave Minnie Spencer a letter to post. Though the envelope was, of course, sealed, the address on the front read: 'Mrs Sach, Claymore House, Hertford Road, East Finchley.' Minnie did indeed post the letter but by now, a number of things were making her grow more and more suspicious of her new tenant.

To begin with, the new-born baby Mrs Walters had brought to the house, seemed to be a very quiet child. She never cried. Further, when Minnie asked if she might hold the child, Mrs Walters rose quickly to her feet, as if in a sort of panic, to prevent her from touching the child and said that she was asleep.

On Saturday 15 November, a second telegram arrived for Mrs Walters. Soon afterwards, Mrs Walters left the house, carrying a bundle, which Minnie Spencer assumed was the baby girl. However, when she returned to the house that evening, at 9.30 pm, Mrs Walters had a different baby, a boy, who she said she was going to take to a woman in South Kensington.

The arrival of these telegrams, the two different babies, and Mrs Walters behaviour had, by now, made Minnie Spencer very suspicious indeed. Fortunately for her, she had other lodgers, two of these were a young couple, Henry and Alice Seal. Even more fortuitously, Henry Seal was a police constable and Minnie took her suspicions to him. He, in turn, reported those suspicions to a superior officer, Detective Inspector Andrew Kyd. On his orders, another constable was set to watch 11 Danbury Street, with instructions to follow Mrs Walters wherever she went.

On Tuesday 18 November, Detective Constable George Wright, was the officer watching the house at Danbury Street. At 9.00 am, he saw Annie Walters leave the house, carrying a bundle with her. Wright then followed her along Knowles Street, and down Rosebery Avenue, where she caught an omnibus. Constable Wright climbed on to the same vehicle and sat some way behind his quarry.

At South Kensington station, Mrs Walters left the omnibus, followed, of course, by Constable Wright. He watched as she paced up and down for a few minutes and then saw her go into the ladies lavatory. Feeling that something might be amiss, Wright then alerted the Station Master, who said that his men would offer whatever assistance the officer might need.

After a few minutes, Annie Walters came out of the lavatory, still carrying the bundle. Fearful that she might have harmed, the child in some way whilst she was inside the toilet, Wright stepped forward, identified himself as a police officer and demanded to see the baby.

Annie asked why he wished to see the child and Wright replied, 'I have reason to believe it is not as it should be.' Annie Walters was then escorted back into the lavatory, where she was seated on a bench, whilst the bundle was unwrapped. Inside, Constable Wright found the dead body of a male baby. Turning back to Walters, he announced, 'I shall now take you in custody on suspicion of murder.'

Annie Walters was taken to King's Cross police station. At 11.00 am, Dr Gaunter was called to the station to make an examination of the baby. Later still, after Annie's lodgings had been searched, Amelia Sach was interviewed, arrested and also taken to King's Cross police station. There, at 10.00 pm that same night, both women were charged with murder.

The trial of twenty-nine-year-old Amelia Sach and fifty-four-year-old Annie Walters opened on 15 January 1903, before Mr Justice Darling, at the Old Bailey. Throughout the two days the proceedings lasted, the case for the Crown was led by Mr Charles Mathews, who was assisted by Mr Bodkin. Amelia Sach was defended by Mr Leycester, whilst Annie Walters was defended by Mr Guy Stephenson.

Some of the early witnesses were called to show that Annie Walters had moved around a good deal and used false names, possibly to impede any potential police investigations. Harry Mann now lived in Roman Road, Ilford but in the autumn of 1902 he had lived at 20 Church Road, Upton Park. From the end of August, until late September 1902, Walters had lodged with him, but at that time she was using the name Mrs Laming.

Elizabeth Lane lived at 7 Crossley Street, Islington. She testified that Annie Walters had lodged with her from 2–29 October, and was then calling herself Mrs Merith. Annie had told her that she worked at Claymore House in Finchley and might be expected a baby to be brought to her by a Mrs Sach.

Thomas William Hood said that he had once lived at 149 Queen's Road, Plaistow and had been a frequent visitor to 20 Glasgow Road. He knew Mrs Laming who lived there, from May 1901 to June 1902. Now, in court, he was able to confirm that Mrs Laming was, in fact, Mrs Walters.

When she had first been arrested, Amelia Sach had denied any knowledge of Annie Walters. The next witness, Eva Brooksby, was the manageress of the Scottish Laundry on Market Parade, Finchley. She knew Sach as a regular customer, when she had lived at 4 Stanley Road, and again when she had moved to Claymore House. Each customer of the laundry had their own reference number, which was written onto the items they brought it. Sach's number was F236. That same number was written on the clothing in which the dead baby was wrapped, showing that it had, at some stage, been with Amelia Sach.

Ada Galley told the court that she had recently given birth to a baby boy. During the birth, which had been a most difficult one, Dr Wylie had been called in to assist and he had used forceps to deliver the child. The following day, Sunday 16 November, Dr Wytlie had returned to examine her again. During the course of that examination, at which Sach was present, he had asked about the baby. Sach had said that Miss Galley's sister had the child, in Holloway. Miss Galley had not corrected her, thinking that perhaps the doctor should not know about the adoption arrangements which had been made. After the doctor had gone, Ada asked Sach where the baby really was and she replied that it had already left the house for its new home.

Rosina Pardoe, like Ada Galley, also worked as a servant at Stanley Villa. She too had become pregnant in 1902 and she too had gone to Claymore House. On 12 November, at 8.30 am, Rosina gave birth to a baby girl. She too had contacted the man who had fathered her child, and he had paid Amelia Sach £30 in the form of two £5 notes and two £10 notes. The two fives were numbered 33192 and 33193, dated 25 August 1902. The two tens were numbered 49172 and 49173 and dated 12 May 1902.

The suggestion of the prosecution was that the baby girl Annie Walters had had with her at Danbury Street, from 12–15 November, was the daughter of Rosina Pardoe and the baby boy she had had from 15–18 November, was the son of Ada Galley. It had been this latter child that Constable Wright had found wrapped in the bundle at South Kensington station.

Dr Alexander Wylie confirmed that he had attended Ada Galley at Claymore House. He also confirmed that he had used forceps to aid the delivery and these may well have left some bruising on the child's head. On 18 November, Dr Wylie had been shown the dead body of a male child. He noticed that there was some bruising about the head and this, along with other factors, led him to believe that the body was that of Miss Galley's son.

After Minnie Spencer had given her evidence, the prosecution called Alice Seal, the wife of the policeman who lodged at Danbury Street. She had fallen into conversation with Mrs Walters soon after she had come to lodge there.

Walters told her that she was a nurse, working for Mrs Sach of Finchley.

Alice Seal also recalled the two babies Mrs Walters had at the house. When the first one was there, Alice had remarked that she seemed to be particularly quiet. Mrs Walters told her that she kept her charges quiet by giving them one or two drops of chlorodyne in their bottles. To this, Alice had exclaimed, 'Oh, be careful. You cannot give a baby as young as that chlorodyne.'

There seemed to be other evidence showing that Annie Walters drugged her charges, possibly killing them soon after she received them. Ethel Jones worked at Lockhart's Coffee Rooms in Whitechapel and she testified that Walters had come into her establishment, on Friday 14 November. She was carrying a bundle and at one stage, part of the shawl fell away to reveal what looked like a child.

The face was very pale indeed and Ethel asked Annie if it were a doll. Annie replied that it was a baby girl under the influence of chloroform, as it had just had an operation. There was no movement whatsoever and, thinking back, Ethel now believed that the child was probably already dead. That child, the prosecution claimed, was the daughter of Rosina Pardoe.

Witnesses were now called to prove the link between the two prisoners. Jessie Bertha Davis was a wardress at Holloway prison and, on 24 November, she had given Sach a piece of paper and asked for a sample of her handwriting. That sample had been given to the next witness, Thomas Henry Gurrin, a handwriting expert, who had compared it with the writing on the two telegrams sent to Annie Walters. In his opinion, the writing was identical, showing that the telegrams had been written by Sach and sent by her.

After constable George Wright had told the court of his arrest of Annie Walters, Detective Inspector Andrew Kyd was called to the stand. He testified that after Walters had been arrested, he went to her lodgings to search them. He had found some items of baby's clothing, a feeding bottle and a small bottle of chlorodyne. From there, he had travelled to Claymore House, with Constable Wright, to see Amelia Sach.

Kyd had announced, 'We are police officers. A woman giving the name of Walters is detained at King's Cross Road police station on suspicion of murdering an infact. I have reason to believe that you have given her the baby.'

Sach had replied; 'I do not know Mrs Walters and I have never given her any babies. I take in ladies to be confined. There is one in my house at present. She was confined last Saturday morning of a baby, a girl. It is with its mother now.'

Sach was then taken to the police station where she saw Walters. She immediately admitted, 'I know the woman. She worked for me but I have never given her any babies.'

Joseph Nespa was the police constable who had charge of the cells at King's Cross, on 18 November. At one stage Walters had called him forward and said she wished to speak to him. Nespa, quite properly, cautioned her and made a note in his pocketbook of what Walters then said. Reading out from his book, Nespa said that Walters had claimed:

> *The child was so cross. I put two drops in its milk and when I woke up in the night, I found the child dead. As for killing that baby, I never did, and if I had got away, I would have drowned myself.*

The last two witnesses were two medical gentlemen. Dr Augustus John Pepper and Dr Richard Lawrence Caunter had performed the post-mortem on the dead boy. They agreed that the child was well nourished and free from any disease which might have caused its death. There was some slight swelling and bruising on the head, almost certainly caused by the use of forceps in the delivery. The child's hands were tightly clenched, suggesting some form of asphyxia. The larynx was congested and the cause of death was suffocation. This would have been due to either the ingestion of a narcotic drug or from direct pressure of a hand over the mouth.

The jury retired to consider their verdict and when it came, it was that both women were guilty of murder, though they did add a recommendation to mercy, on account of the two defendants being women. The law, however, only had one penalty available and both women were sentenced to death.

There was to be no reprieve, and on Tuesday 3 February 1903, Amelia Sach and Annie Walters were hanged at Holloway prison, by William Billington and Henry Pierrepoint. They were the first ever executions at Holloway and this was the only occasion in the twentieth century, where two women were hanged together.

# CHAPTER 22

# Clara Alice White
# 1912

S ome of the crimes within the pages of this book made headlines across the world. Others certainly caused much newsprint to be used, within the United Kingdom, but there were other stories involving family tragedies, which were just as important for those who were involved. One such case was that of Clara Alice White.

Clara was a married woman with two beautiful children: Patrick John, who was aged three and a half and Lilian May, who was almost two years old. In the early part of 1912, Clara's husband left her, but it wasn't long before she moved in with Walter Risley at 30 Raynham Road, Edmonton.

Walter, too, was married, but he had separated from his wife some seven years before. By all accounts he was very fond of Clara and her two children and, for a time at least, the new family appeared to be very happy together, sharing one room upstairs and one downstairs, in the house in Raynham Road.

Clara, however, was a worrier and when Walter had an accident at work, it added to those worries. Still, he did receive some weekly compensation so, at least for the time being, there were no real financial concerns. Unfortunately, in September, that compensation stopped and that was something else for Clara to worry about.

On Monday 30 September, Clara rose from her bed at the usual time, in order to see to her children. Walter Risley got up a little later and was immediately greeted by Clara demanding to know how they were going to pay the rent that week. Walter told her not to worry and then, at around 10.30 am, he left the house to meet up with Clara's brother, Alfred Wackett.

Despite the fact that money was something of a problem, Walter and Alfred visited the *Bricklayer's Arms*, where they enjoyed a pint together. Around half an hour later, at approximately 11.00 am, Clara came into the pub herself and, after a brief chat with the two men, took some beer back with her to have with lunch later.

Walter Risley arrived back at Raynham Road at 12.15 pm. At that time, Clara was at home with the two children, but there was also a neighbour present, who had brought her child with her. As Walter and Clara sat down to lunch, the children were playing and being rather noisy. Walter suggested that they should be allowed to go out and play in the passageway, so that the adults could have their meal in peace. To his surprise, Clara objected to this and a full-blown argument soon developed between them. In an attempt to avoid confrontation, Walter went upstairs to bed, after he had finished eating.

At around 2.00 pm, a half-asleep Walter was roused by a loud cry of, 'I've done it!' Such was the tone of the cry that it alarmed Walter and he dashed downstairs to see what the problem might be.

Even as he was rushing downstairs, Walter saw Clara leave the house by the front door. He followed her and saw that she was hammering on the front door of the house next door, number 28, where Harriett Dolladay lived. Concerned now for the whereabouts of the two children, Walter went back inside his own house and into the front room.

The youngest child, Lilian, was in her cot, sitting up and screaming in agony. The boy, Patrick, was rolling about the floor, also screaming and also in obvious pain. Even as Walter took in this awful scene, Clara came into the room, bringing Mrs Dolladay with her.

Harriett Dolladay could see that both children were foaming at the mouth and it was plain that some kind of poison had been given to them. As she and Walter tried to counter the effects of this, by giving them salt dissolved in water, Clara calmly announced, 'I'll go and find a policeman and give myself up.'

Clara did not have to walk very far before she found Constable Charles Wade. By the time he escorted Clara back to the house, Walter had run off to get the doctor. He returned soon afterwards with Dr John Shaw whose practice was situated at 216 Fore Street.

As soon as Dr Shaw arrived, Constable Wade, who had by now made a quick search of the living room, handed him a bottle he had found. The bottle was labelled, 'Spirits of Salt, Poison'; and it was reasonable to assume that substance, otherwise known as Hydrochloric Acid, was what had been administered to both children.

The children were both still in acute pain. Dr Shaw gave them both a solution of Carbonate of Soda and then had them removed to the Edmonton Infirmary. It was, however, too late, and both children died that same evening. Clara White was now facing two charges of murder.

Clara White faced her trial at the Old Bailey, on 8 October 1912. As is customary in British courts, only one charge was proceeded with, that of murdering Patrick, her son.

After Walter Risley had given his evidence, the prosecution called Harriett Dolladay. She testified that she had seen Clara two or three times on the fateful day of 30 September. Clara seemed to be perfectly normal, but then, that afternoon, there was a loud and persistent hammering on Harriett's front door. As she opened it, Clara almost fell into her arms. She was hysterical and screamed out, 'I've done my children in.' She was screaming and throwing herself about the room. Harriett went next door with Clara and saw the children crying out in pain and foaming from the mouth. She then heard Clara announce that she was going to give herself up to the police, as Walter tried to make the children sick by giving them salt water.

Constable Wade said that he had been on patrol in Fore Street, on the afternoon of 30 September, when the prisoner had rushed up to him and said, 'I have killed them. I have poisoned them.' Wade asked who she might be talking about and Clara had replied, 'My two children.' Wade had then taken her back to her home and sent Walter Risley off to fetch the doctor before he made a search of the premises. It was Constable Wade and another officer, who arrived shortly afterwards, who carried the two stricken children to the hospital.

Dr Basil Eustace Moss had performed the post-mortems on both children, on 30 September. He confirmed that both deaths were due to the administration of a corrosive poison and this was consistent with the use of Hydrochloric Acid. The mouths and lips of both children were badly burned. That same night, Dr Moss had also examined Clara at the police station. She was extremely hysterical and though she did smell of drink, Dr Moss would not say that she was drunk or under the influence of alcohol.

George Henry Hamilton was an assistant at a chemist's shop at 123 Fore Street, Edmonton. He testified that, at 10.30 am on the morning of 30 September, Clara had come into his shop with an empty bottle and asked for two pence worth of Spirits of Salt, which he had supplied.

The final piece of evidence was a report from the medical officer of Holloway prison, where Clara had been held after her arrest. He had observed Clara since she had been received at the prison and also examined her family history. It appeared that in 1906, Clara's father, George Wackett, had committed suicide by cutting his own throat. Of more importance though, was his report on Clara herself. In that report, the conclusion was that Clara was suffering from a good deal of mental confusion and was not in a condition to realise the nature and quality of the act she had committed. However, the report also stated that, although Clara had been of unsound mind at the time she killed her children, her condition had improved since and she was fit to plead to the charges against her.

The matter was now up to the jury and, in the event, they decided that Clara was guilty, but insane. Clara was thus spared the death sentence and committed to an asylum for treatment.

# CHAPTER 23

# Marie Marguerite Alibert Fahmy
# 1923

ohn Paul Beattie was the night porter at the famous *Savoy Hotel* and at 2.30 am, on the morning of Tuesday 10 July 1923, he was taking luggage up to room 50 on the fourth-floor Savoy Court.

As Beattie approached suite number 41, the door opened and the occupant, Prince Ali Hamel Bey, came out, pointing up at his face. 'Look at my face. Look what she has done,' cried the Prince. Beattie saw that there was indeed a mark, albeit very slight, on Bey's left cheek. Even as Beattie stood before the Prince, that gentleman's wife, Madam Marie Fahmy, followed her husband out of the suite and stood framed in the doorway. She too began to talk and point to her face but since she was speaking in French, Beattie had no idea what she was saying. The Prince listened to what his wife was saying and then asked Beattie to call for the night manager. Beattie did as he had been asked, and then went on his way to room 50.

As Beattie approached room 50 with the luggage, three loud reports rang out. Certain that those reports had been shots, Beattie dropped the luggage and dashed back towards suite 41. As he arrived there, Beattie saw that the Prince was now lying against a wall, in the corridor, outside room 42, bleeding badly from his head. As for his wife, Madam Fahmy, she stood before her husband and, as Beattie watched, dropped a revolver on the floor. Beattie immediately picked up the weapon and, for safety's sake, placed it inside a luggage lift, some three yards away. Even as he did so, Madam Fahmy followed and Beattie then caught hold of her. She said something to him, again in French, but after a few seconds she managed to say the one word 'cloak' and pointed back inside her suite. Beattie took this to mean that Madam Fahmy wanted her cloak, so he briefly went inside the suite, found the cloak, and then gave it to the shocked woman. Beattie then rang down for the manager, Mr Marini.

Arthur Marini, the night manager, soon arrived at the scene of the shooting. Madam Fahmy was still talking but fortunately, Marini did speak French. She said to him, 'What shall I do? I have shot him.' Taking charge, Marini then told Beattie to telephone the police at the Bow Street station, and also to call for an ambulance, the hotel's general manager and the hotel's doctor. Marini then gently escorted Madam Fahmy back into her suite, to await their arrival. During this time, Madam Fahmy continued to speak, in French, saying, 'What will they do with me? We were quarrelling over my divorce that was to take place shortly in Paris. You see, I have all my tickets ready and I was leaving for Paris tomorrow. What will my children do?'

It was clear that Madam Fahmy had shot her husband. When he died from his injuries, at 3.25 am that same morning, she was charged with wilful murder.

Madam Fahmy appeared at the Old Bailey, on 10 September 1923, before Mr Justice Swift, to answer that charge. The trial lasted until 15 September, during which time the case for the prosecution was led by Mr Percival Clarke, assisted by Mr Eustace Fulton. Madam Fahmy was defended by the redoubtable Sir Edward Marshall Hall who was assisted by Sir Henry Curtis Bennett, and Mr Rowland Oliver.

During the early part of the trial, some of the personal history of Madam Fahmy was detailed. She had been born Marie Marguerite Alibert, in Paris, on 9 December 1890. When she was still only sixteen, on 21 January 1907, Marie had given birth to a daughter, whom she named Raymonde. In March 1919, she had married a man named Charles Laurent, in Venice, but the relationship was not a happy one and they had divorced, in Paris, on 30 March 1920.

Marie continued to live in that city and it was there, on 8 May 1922, that she had met Prince Ali Hamel Bey, who was in Paris on holiday. There appeared to be an instant attraction between the two and a romance soon developed. They became lovers and travelled to Italy, Deauville, and Biarritz. An engagement was announced and, in December 1922, they married in Cairo, afterwards living in the Prince's palace on the banks of the River Nile. Initially, the age difference between the two did not seem to matter. By now, of course, Marie was thirty-two, whilst the Prince was only twenty-three but, in due course, the relationship began to grow more and more strained. There were a large number of arguments, some of them quite violent and Marie began to sleep with a revolver beneath her pillow. On 18 May 1923, the couple had returned to Paris where they stayed at the *Hotel Majestic*. Then, on 1 July, they had travelled to London with their staff, and taken rooms at the *Savoy*.

One of the early witnesses was Said Enamy, who had been the Prince's secretary for some five years. He had been one of the staff members, who had travelled to London with the couple and he had been given room 127.

Said testified that on the afternoon of 9 July 1923, he had taken lunch with Madam Fahmy and the Prince. During the meal, they had been throwing insults at each other and at one stage Madam Fahmy had told her husband that she intended to leave him, adding that he would pay dearly for it. After lunch, Said had retired to his room for a time, but later that day he had accompanied Madam Fahmy on a shopping trip. They returned to the hotel at around 5.00 pm.

That evening, Said, Madam Fahmy and the Prince had all gone to Daly's Theatre, on Cranbourne Street, where they saw a performance of *The Merry Widow*, after which they had returned to the *Savoy*, where they all had supper together. After this, they adjourned to the ballroom but Madam Fahmy had refused to dance with her husband, though she had danced with Said.

At 1.30 am, on 10 July, Said had escorted Madam Fahmy to the lift so that she could go up to her suite. He then returned to the Prince and the two men spoke about the problems he was having with the marriage. It was 2.00 am by the time the Prince bade his secretary goodnight, and retired to his room. Less than an hour later, the telephone rang in Said's room. It was Madam Fahmy and she said, in French, 'I have shot Ali.

Come down immediately.' Said had then gone to the suite where he had found his master lying in the corridor, bleeding badly from a wound in his head.

Sergeant George Hall was one of the first police officers on the scene and he told the court that when he arrived, the Prince was lying on his right side, on the floor in the corridor, outside the suite. The Prince was wearing a light, white, night-shirt, a dressing gown and slippers. Soon afterwards, Dr Gordon arrived and he joined Sergeant Hall in Suite 41 where Madame Fahmy spoke to them. Sergeant Hall did not speak French but Dr Gordon did and he translated. Apparently, Madam Fahmy admitted that she had shot her husband and, as a porter handed a revolver over to Hall, she went on to say, 'That is the weapon I did it with.'

Sergeant Hall made a quick search of the bedroom but could find no traces of blood, which indicated that the Prince had been shot in the corridor outside. Madam Fahmy then asked him if she might be permitted to change, since she was still wearing an evening dress. Permission was granted and, soon afterwards, she was escorted to Bow Street police station, for formal interview.

Dr Edward Francis Strathearn Gordon told the court that he had been attending Madam Fahmy for a week prior to the shooting. She had complained to him about suffering from haemorrhoids and, in all, he had seen her six or seven times. On her last visit to his surgery, on 9 July, Dr Gordon had arranged for her to see a specialist and the result of that consultation was that she was due to go into a nursing home, for an operation, on 10 July. Of course, the death of her husband meant that she was unable to keep that appointment.

After the shooting, Dr Gordon had been called out to the hotel. Later still, he went with her to the police station and continued to act as interpreter. It was at Bow Street that she explained that, after seeing him on 9 July, and agreeing to the operation, she had returned to the hotel and told her husband what had transpired. He had told her that she was not to have any operation in London. An argument developed during which she said that she would leave him, whereupon he threatened to kill her if she did. He also threatened to smash her head in with a bottle.

During the early hours of 10 July, when the Prince had come up to the suite, he had advanced towards her, in the bedroom, in a threatening manner, and she had run to the bed and snatched up her revolver, for protection. She turned and fired one shot out of the open window, in order to frighten him, but he continued to advance upon her. She tried to escape and they ran out into the corridor where she pointed the gun at him and fired several times. He fell down, and at first she thought he was shamming, until she saw the blood.

Dr Gordon had also performed the post-mortem on the dead Prince and now detailed the wounds he had found. The first wound was a small, circular wound on the left temple and this was described as an entrance wound. Next, there was a two-inch-wide wound behind the right ear, which Dr Gordon described as an exit wound.

The third wound was slightly larger than the second, and positioned below the lobule of the left ear. This too, was an exit wound. Next, there was a small circular wound on the left arm. Another small wound lay on the inner side of the left arm, with a sixth at the same level in the thoracic wall. The seventh, and final wound was in the back, on the left side, one and a half inches below the lower angle of the scapula.

In effect, Madam Fahmy's defence was two-fold. The first was that her husband was abusive to her, and that there had been a number of heated arguments between them during their stormy marriage. The second line of defence was that he had demanded that she perform unnatural sexual acts; that is that throughout their marriage, he had insisted on anal sex, and that this had been the direct cause of the haemorrhoids.

Part of her testimony was backed up by two witnesses. Aimee Pain was Madam Fahmy's personal maid. She had started working for her in October 1922. She said that she was a witness to many arguments between the couple and she had seen the Prince assault her mistress many times.

Ellen Dryland was a chambermaid at the *Savoy*. She testified that, on either 5 July, or 6 July, whilst cleaning the suite, she had found a revolver beneath the bolster of the bed. She had put the weapon into the drawer of a small bedside table, for safety. After the shooting, once the scene had been released by the police, Ellen had cleaned the room and found a spent cartridge case, near the open window, by that same bedside table. It seemed that Madam Fahmy had been telling the truth when she referred to firing a warning shot out of the hotel window.

There were, however, two other witnesses, whose testimony appeared to show that this was a premeditated act of murder. Mahmoud Abdul Fath, was a close friend of both the Prince and Madam Fahmy and she had spoken freely to him about her marital problems. During one conversation she had confessed that she hated Ali and had a plan, or programme, which she was going to put into action in London. Though she never actually said what the plan was, Fath believed that she intended to kill her husband.

Fanny Luis ran a dress shop in Cairo and Madam Fahmy was a regular customer. Again she spoke openly about her marriage and told Fanny that Ali constantly wished to engage in an unnatural vice. Yet again, Madam Fahmy said that she had a plan, which would free her, and which she intended to carry out once they were in Europe.

The time came for Madam Fahmy to take the stand herself. Sir Edward Marshall Hall, concentrating on the so-called debauched life the Prince had led, guided his client carefully through the indignities which she said she had been forced to suffer. Surprisingly, the prosecution was then not allowed to cross-examine her, as to whether she too had led an immoral life. Had they been allowed to, the jury might well have heard of her illegitimate daughter, and the fact that there was evidence that Marie had then become a prostitute and also had lesbian tendencies.

The jury took less than an hour to decide that, not only was Marie Fahmy not guilty of murder, but she was not guilty of manslaughter either. She had killed in self-defence and was therefore a free woman.

Marie returned to Paris after the trial, where she discovered that she had no claim to her dead husband's fortune. A few years later, she tried to claim that she had been pregnant at the time she shot her husband, had borne a son, and he was therefore entitled to his father's estate. The claim was dismissed out of hand and Marie became something of a recluse, treated as a laughing stock by society. She never married again and died alone, in Paris, on 2 January 1971. She was eighty years of age.

# CHAPTER 24

# Styllou Pantopiou Christofi
# 1954

Harry Burstoff, who lived at 8 Oman Avenue, was driving down South Hill Park, towards Hampstead Railway Station, at around 12.50 am, on Thursday 29 July 1954, with his wife in the front passenger seat. Harry and his wife were chatting with each other when, suddenly, a woman ran out into the road, signalling for him to stop, and shouting, 'Taxi! Taxi!'

Harry stopped his car and rolled down his window. The woman approached and, in broken English, blurted out, 'Please come. Fire burning. Babies sleeping.' Then, before Harry could ask the woman what had happened, she dashed off back up the hill. Thinking that the woman might need his help, Harry turned his car around and followed her.

Even as Harry craned his neck to see where the woman was heading, she suddenly turned and ran up the steps, which led to number 11. The front door there was open and there was a light on in the hallway. Not sure exactly what he should do next, Harry tentatively followed the woman inside. The woman was waiting, just inside the hallway and Harry asked, 'Where's the fire?' The woman put a finger to her lips and replied, 'Ssh, babies are sleeping.'

As Harry's wife, Fanny Burstoff, made her own way up the steps, the mysterious woman opened another door and vanished into one of the other rooms. Before Harry could venture after her, his wife called out, 'Look, there's somebody on the floor.'

There was indeed someone lying on the floor, in the entrance to the yard at the back of the house. As Harry and his wife moved closer, they could see that whoever that was, they were beyond all help. Not only was there a good deal of blood about the person's head, but the body was badly burnt. As the strange woman came back to where Harry and his wife stood, Harry announced that he would have to telephone for the police.

The woman who had stopped his car in the street, pointed to a telephone. Harry had actually no idea where he was and asked her what the address was. She seemed to understand because, although she did not reply, she took him to the front door and pointed out the number. Then she handed him an envelope from a letter rack. This gave the name Christofi and the address of 11 South Park Avenue. Harry then telephoned the police and waited outside, with his wife, for them to arrive.

At 1.26 am, Sergeant Maurice Stevens was on duty in Cricklewood Broadway when he received a message to go to South Hill Park. On arrival at number 11, he found Harry and Fanny Burstoff outside and they told him, briefly, what had happened. Sergeant Stevens then went inside the house and found the woman who had summoned Burstoff to the body, which was lying nearby, just inside the yard. Sergeant Stevens then tried to question the woman, but she would only reply, 'I no speak. I no understand.'

Sergeant Edward Welch arrived at the scene at 1.45 am. He, too, tried to question the woman, but could get no sensible answers from her. By now, his colleague, Sergeant Stevens, had discovered that there were children asleep upstairs. Welch managed to signal to the woman that she should go upstairs and look after them. She nodded and did as she was told.

Within moments of Sergeant Welch's arrival, Dr Philip Hopkins also attended. He confirmed that the body was that of a young woman, who was dead. He noted too that there was a strong smell of paraffin around the body and in the yard itself. There was also a good deal of water around the body, possibly indicating that an attempt had been made to douse the flames.

The pathologist, Dr Francis Edward Camps, arrived at the scene at 5.00 am. He noted that the body was that of a slim, well-nourished female, who had been approximately five feet four inches tall. She was naked, apart from a pair of what looked like shorts. Her tongue was sticking out from between her teeth, which possibly indicated asphyxia, and her hair was soaked in dried blood.

Later that same day, Dr Camps performed the post-mortem which revealed that there were no carbon particles in the victim's lungs or air passages, indicating that she had been dead before she was doused in paraffin, which was then set alight. The woman's skull was fractured across the back and the wound showed that she had been struck with some round, linear object. The woman's nose was also broken, but the direct cause of death was strangulation. It appeared that she had been hit over the head with something heavy, which may have rendered her unconscious. She was then strangled to death, soaked in paraffin and set alight.

By now, names had been put to the people involved in this tragedy. The house was occupied by the Christofi family. The head of the house was Stavros Pantopiou Christofi, who was a Greek Cypriot. He had come to Britain in 1937 and five years later, in 1942, he had married a German girl, Hella Dorothea Bleicher.

The union was a happy one and the couple had had three children, two boys and one girl, who were now aged between nine and twelve years. In July 1953, Stavros' mother, Styllou, had come to England from Cyprus, but it was clear from the outset that she and Hella did not get along.

Over the next year, the atmosphere at South Hill Park grew worse and worse until, finally, Hella told Stavros that she thought it would be better if his mother returned to Cyprus. This was talked about at length and, finally, a decision was made. On 12 August, Hella was due to go for a holiday to Germany, taking the children with her to meet their relatives over there. When she returned, Styllou would see her grandchildren for the last time and then she would be sent back home. This would certainly have taken place before the winter set in.

Stavros was a wine waiter at the *Café Royal* in London's West End, and it was there that the police called to inform him that all was not well at home and he should return at once. His wife, thirty-six-year old Hella, was the dead woman whose burnt body had been found in the yard and his mother, fifty-three-year-old Styllou, the one who had flagged down Harry Burstoff's car, was the person accused of killing her.

The trial of Styllou Pantopiou Christofi took place at the Old Bailey, on 28 October 1954, with the case for the prosecution resting in the redoubtable hands of Mr Christmas Humphreys.

The first witness was Detective Constable William Carter who had gone to 11 South Hill Park, on 29 July, to take some photographs of the scene. Later that same day, he had gone to the mortuary at St Pancras to take further pictures of the deceased. Some of those photographs are reproduced in the plates section of this book.

Stavros Christofi told the court of the problems between his wife and mother. Styllou, it seemed, was of the old-school and was constantly telling Hella how she should be bringing her children up. This led to constant arguments between the two, which had culminated in Styllou being told that she would have to go back to Cyprus.

On the night his wife had died, Stavros had gone to work at 8.30 pm, which was the last time he had seen his wife alive. At 3.00 am on the 29th, the police had called the restaurant and told him that he needed to go home. He arrived there at 3.30 am to find his wife dead and the police waiting for him. Stavros was asked to act as translator whilst the police asked Styllou some questions. As he told the officers what his mother said, it was written down and later Styllou put her mark on the paper.

Stavros, however, had one more important piece of evidence to give.

A pair of French windows led out to the yard where Hella's body had been found. They were not capable of being locked, so Hella had come up with the idea of placing a large garden fork beneath the handle, at night, to secure them. When the police and others had arrived at the scene, that fork had been found next to the doorway. This would prove crucial when Styllou's statement to the police was read out later.

Eric Porter was a partner in Fashion Ways Limited, a clothing company who traded from premises at St George's

Street. He confirmed that Hella had worked for his company, since 3 July 1953 and was a valued employee. She always seemed to be happy, doted on her family and was very happy with her husband.

Robert William Cooper now lived at 1 Frognal Close, but in July 1945, he had moved into the second floor flat at 11 South Hill Park, where he remained until October 1953. He knew the Christofi family very well and had been back to visit them a number of times since he had moved. His last visit was on the evening of Wednesday 28 July, the evening Hella was attacked. Robert had arrived there at 9.35 pm and only stayed for five minutes or so. When he left, Hella was alive and well. He had not seen any sign of Styllou that night.

John Byres Young lived next door but one to the Christofis, at number 15 South Hill Park. At some time between 11.30 pm and 11.45 pm, on 28 July, he had gone into his back garden with his dog. Immediately he noticed an orange glow from the garden of number 11, as if there was someone burning something.

Curious as to what could be happening, John called out but there was no reply from number 11. He then called his wife, Thomasina, who came out to take a look for herself. As she waited in her own yard, John crossed the intervening yard and looked over the wall into the yard of number 11. There was indeed a fire, which appeared to be a wax model. There was also a very strong smell of paraffin. As he watched, John saw Styllou come out and bend over the burning figure and had the impression that she was about to stir the fire up. Seeing no reason to interfere, John returned to his own yard and told his wife what he had seen.

After Harry and Fanny Burstoff had given their evidence, a number of police officers, including Sergeant Stevens and Sergeant Welch, gave their testimony. They were followed by medical evidence, given by Dr Hopkins and Dr Camps.

Albert Evans, another police officer, had searched the premises on 30 July. At one stage he had noticed that a clock on the mantelpiece in the back bedroom appeared to have been recently moved. Taking it down, Evans found a small cellophane parcel behind it and, upon unwrapping this, found a gold wedding ring. This had since been identified as belonging to Hella Christofi. The bedroom in which it was found, was that of Styllou.

Styllou did not speak English very well, her native tongue being Greek. When she had been interviewed by Detective Inspector Robert Fenwick, at Hampstead police station, the services of an interpreter, Mr Christodoulous Protopapa, had been provided. According to Styllou's statement, she had been asleep in bed when she had been woken by the smell of smoke. Upon investigating, she had found Hella's body ablaze in the yard and had thrown water over it in an attempt to save her. Someone must have broken into the house and attacked Hella.

Unfortunately for Styllou this did not explain how the garden fork had been moved to the side of the French windows, how Hella's wedding ring, which she never took off, had found its way into Styllou's bedroom or why John Young had seen her merely looking over the body.

There was, perhaps, just one hope for Styllou. Dr Christie was the Chief Medical Officer at Holloway prison and he had been observing the prisoner since her incarceration there. He noted that she had had very little schooling, was hysterical, distressed, restless and aggressive. She spent some nights just sitting up in bed, screaming. Dr Christie had come to the conclusion that Styllou was mentally deranged. However, curiously, although his report clearly stated that Styllou was insane, it went on to say that she was fit to plead to the charge and stand trial.

In the event, the jury chose to dismiss the suggestion of insanity and found Styllou guilty as charged. Only now could it be revealed that, in 1926, when she was just twenty-five years old, Styllou had been charged with murder in her native Cyprus. She had, apparently, killed her mother-in-law, by ramming a burning torch down her throat. On that charge, she had been found not guilty!

An appeal was heard, and dismissed, on 29 November. Exactly sixteen days later, on Wednesday 15 December 1954,

Styllou Christofi was hanged at Holloway by Albert Pierrepoint. As a member of the Greek Orthodox church, Styllou had asked that a cross from her faith should be placed in the execution chamber so that it would be the last thing she should see. The request was granted and the cross remained until the cell was dismantled in 1967. That meant that only one more condemned woman, the subject of the next chapter, would ever see that cross.

# CHAPTER 25

# Ruth Ellis
# 1955

On 9 October 1926, Bertha Neilson presented her husband Arthur with a new baby daughter, whom they named Ruth. At the time, the family lived at 74 West Parade, Rhyl but a few years later, in 1933, they moved to Basingstoke in Hampshire.

In 1940, when she was fourteen years old, Ruth Neilson left school and, the following year, the family moved to Southwark, in London. Soon after this, their home was bombed in the German air-raids and the Neilsons were forced to move yet again, this time, to 19 Francis Road, Camberwell. Ruth was, by now, earning her living working at the OXO factory in Southwark but, in March 1942, she was diagnosed with rheumatic fever and spent a few months in hospital, being finally discharged, on 3 May 1942.

Ruth Neilson was not happy working at the factory, and wanted more from life. In due course she found herself a new position, as a photographer's assistant. It was whilst working for him that one night she met a French-Canadian airman whose surname was Clare. An affair followed, Ruth found herself pregnant and, on 15 September 1944, gave birth to a son who she named Clare Andria Neilson. Unfortunately, there was no chance of a long lasting relationship with the father, as he had a wife and family back in Canada.

Ruth still hadn't found her niche in life and other career moves followed. First, she found herself a job as a cashier in a café, but that didn't satisfy her. Then she became a model at a camera club where she was paid the sum of £1 an hour, more than she had ever earned before. This was more Ruth's style and she loved the glamour of the business. As part of that glamour, Ruth and her clique of friends used to spend a good deal of time at the Court Club in Duke Street and it was there that she first met the club owner, Morris Conley.

Ruth first met Conley in 1946. They hit it off from the outset and it wasn't long before Conley offered Ruth a position as a hostess at the club, at a wage of £5 per week. More than that, there were customers to entertain and some of them were very generous indeed. They spent money freely and, since Ruth was on ten percent commission on sales, her income grew accordingly.

It was at the Court Club that Ruth Neilson first met a man who would change her name, to one of the most infamous in British criminal history. George Johnston Ellis was recently divorced. They met at a time when Ruth was somewhat fragile emotionally, as she had just undergone an abortion. A relationship developed, and the couple married on 8 November 1950.

Though the marriage was not a happy one, Ruth did get pregnant again and, on 2 October 1951, gave birth to a daughter, Georgina. Just one month later, Ruth and George split and she returned to her parents' house, with the two children. Ruth didn't stay there long, however. She did leave her son and her daughter with her parents, but Ruth contacted Morris Conley again. By now, the Court Club had been renamed Carroll's but Conley was happy to take Ruth back as a hostess. Indeed, he was also happy to install Ruth in her own place, at Flat 4, Gilbert Court, Oxford Street. In fact, the only thing that seemed to have changed, was Ruth's name. Though she had parted from her husband, Ruth would, from now on, be known to all by her new name, Ruth Ellis.

It was at Carroll's, in 1953, that Ruth Ellis met two new men, who would play crucial roles in her life: Desmond Cussen and David Moffat Drummond Blakely. Both men were racing car enthusiasts and, at least at this stage, quite good friends. The first meeting with Blakely was anything but auspicious. He behaved in a most boorish manner and insulted some of Ruth's fellow hostesses. Ruth gave as good as she got and told Blakely, in no uncertain terms, precisely what she thought of him.

It was in October 1953 that Morris Conley gave Ruth a new job. Now, she was promoted to manageress of another of his clubs, The Little Club, situated at 17 Brompton Road, Knightsbridge. Not only was Ruth in charge, but she was also given the flat over the club. No sooner had she taken over, than one of her first customers was David Blakely.

This time, however, his behaviour was totally different. He was charming, amusing and witty. Whereas before, Ruth had found him to be nothing more than obnoxious, now she was fascinated by him. Within a week, they were lovers. This did little to please Desmond Cussen, who was also attracted to Ruth, and the early stages of animosity between the two men, began to grow.

David Blakely, as was previously stated, was interested in motor cars and racing. With a business partner, Anthony Findlater, he was in the process of building a new racing car, which they, rather grandly, had named *The Emperor*. Unfortunately, building, testing, and racing the car proved to be a severe financial drain on Blakely's resources. These financial concerns led, in turn, to temper tantrums and these meant that the new relationship with Ruth was, to say the least, volatile.

There was also the fact that, occasionally, David appeared to be ashamed of Ruth. He certainly did not believe that his parents would approve of her. On one occasion, David had driven Ruth to Penn in Buckinghamshire, where his parents lived. David called in at the local public house, only to find that his mother was already inside with some family friends. Instead of introducing his lover to his mother, David told Ruth to stay in the car and brought a drink out to her. Rather surprisingly, perhaps, Ruth did not argue and did as she was asked.

As a racing fanatic, one of the high points of the year for David Blakely was the twenty-four-hours Le Man race. In June 1954, David went to the race as a co-driver. However, he did not return to Ruth when he had said he would. This time, Ruth would not calmly accept this snub. She gained her revenge by taking Desmond Cussen to bed. When David found out about this, he was furious, but the blazing argument that ensued did not split Ruth Ellis and David Blakely. If anything, it threw them even closer together and they soon patched up the argument, in bed.

Meanwhile, Morris Conley had noticed that the takings at The Little Club, were falling. This might well have been due to the fact that Ruth's mind was more on Blakely, than business, but Morris was not to be cajoled. In October 1954, he fired Ruth, which meant that she also lost the flat above the club. Desmond Cussen suggested that she move in with him at Goodwood Court, Devonshire Street. This led, once again, to a massive row between her and David.

Ruth lived with Desmond until February 1955, which put an extreme strain on her continuing relationship with David. After much discussion about their future, David suggested that they should get a place together. This was precisely what Ruth had wanted all along and she was deliriously happy, when she and David moved into a flat together, at 44 Egerton Gardens. Ruth and David took the lease as Mr and Mrs Ellis.

It might well be said that Ruth and David could not live apart, but equally, they could not live together. Even though they were now living in the same flat, the relationship was as tempestuous as ever. One moment they were at each other's throats, the next they would be making love. Things were, however, moving towards some sort of crisis. That crisis came in April 1955.

On Saturday 2 April 1955, David Blakely entered *The Emperor* into a car race. Unfortunately, the vehicle blew up during the race. David's already frayed temper was not helped by Ruth trying to console him. He turned on her, shouted that she was some kind of jinx, and blamed her for the problems with the car. Ruth was rather fragile emotionally as she had only recently discovered that she was pregnant once again. Back at the flat, the couple argued yet again. So heated did this argument become that, at one stage, David struck out at Ruth and hit her in the stomach. Ruth lost her baby and was unwell until Tuesday 5 April.

David's racing partner, Anthony Findlater, lived at 29 Tanza Road, Hampstead, with his wife, Carole. Before the Findlaters had married, David had known Carole and the two had been lovers. Ruth knew about this and the knowledge that David and Carole had once been together, did not improve her state of mind that April.

On Friday 8 April, which happened to be Good Friday, David had been out with the Findlaters, drinking at the *Magdala Tavern* on South Hill Park. That evening, David had agreed to call for Ruth but, as he drank with his friends and brooded on the way his relationship with Ruth had been of late, David changed his mind. He simply couldn't face Ruth that night and told Carole that he wished he had the courage to make the final break from her. Concerned that their friend had nowhere else to go, the Findlaters suggested that David spend that Easter weekend with them, in Tanza Road. A relieved David readily accepted the offer. However, he did not bother to let Ruth know of his change of plans.

At 8.30 pm that evening, a worried Ruth telephoned the Findlaters. The telephone was picked up by Anthony. Ruth said that she was very worried. David was supposed to be home by now and he hadn't even telephoned her. When she asked Anthony if David were at Tanza Road, he denied it. Ruth did not believe him, so her next telephone call was to Desmond Cussen, who she asked to drive her from Egerton Gardens to the Findlater's flat.

Cussen agreed to the request and, when Ruth arrived at Tanza Road, she saw David's station wagon parked outside the flat. Now she knew the truth. David was with the Findlaters, they had lied to her and perhaps there was something after all in her suspicions that the relationship with Carole wasn't really over after all.

Ruth rang the doorbell but there was no reply. Finding a telephone box, she then rang the Findlater's flat again but as soon as they recognised her voice, they hung up on her. A furious Ruth returned to Desmond Cussen's car, took his rubber coated torch, returned to David's car and pushed in some of the windows. The police were called and they strongly advised Ruth to go home. She did, but not until 2.00 am.

After catching up on some long overdue sleep, Ruth telephoned the Findlaters again on the morning of Saturday 9 April. Once again, the receiver was replaced once her voice was recognised. Later that same day, Desmond Cussen drove Ruth back to Tanza Road and she then spent some hours, a little further down the street, watching the flat. That evening, Ruth saw that there was a party going on at the flat. Then, at around 10.00 pm, she finally saw David emerge, with an attractive woman on his arm. A distraught Ruth made her lonely way home.

Ruth spent much of Sunday 10 April, brooding on what had happened over the last few days. Meanwhile, back at Tanza Road, Carole Findlater had run out of cigarettes. It was David who volunteered to get some from the *Magdala Tavern*. A friend of his, Bertram Clive Gunnell, who preferred to use his middle name, said that he would accompany David down there, and perhaps they might have a drink whilst they were there. The two men left together at around 8.30 pm.

Approximately one hour later, at 9.30 pm, David and Clive left the public house. Clive walked to the front passenger seat whilst David fumbled for his car keys and strode around to the driver's side, carrying some bottles of beer. As David rummaged through his pockets, a blonde woman stepped forward and spoke his name.

It is almost certain that David Blakely knew that the woman who had called him, was Ruth, but he chose to ignore her. He didn't notice as Ruth reached into her handbag and brought out a .38 Smith and Wesson revolver, calling his name once more as she did so.

This time, David did react. He turned to face Ruth and, for the first time, noticed the gun in her hand. As he dashed back and tried to run around the back of the car, Ruth fired twice into his fleeing form. David fell on the pavement, close to the newsagent's shop, next door to the *Magdala*. Ruth then stood over him and fired two more shots into his body.

In all, Ruth Ellis fired six shots. One bullet missed completely, four struck David Blakely, and the final one ricocheted off the wall of the *Magdala* and struck Gladys Kensington Yule who was walking, with her husband. Ruth, though, knew none of this, for she was still pointing the gun at David's prone figure, and pulling the trigger repeatedly. The click of the hammer on the empty chambers was all that could now be heard.

Having heard all the commotion outside, customers of the *Magdala* ran outside to see what had happened. A dazed Ruth turned to one of the customers and asked him to call the police. The man, Alan Thompson, identified himself as an off duty constable, carefully took the revolver from Ruth, and placed her under arrest.

Ruth Ellis' trial for murder opened at the Old Bailey, on 20 June 1955, before Mr Justice Havers. Throughout the two days of the proceedings, the case for the Crown was led by Mr Christmas Humphreys, who was assisted by Mr Mervyn Griffith-Jones and Miss Jean Southwood. Ruth's defence was led by Mr Melford Stevenson, assisted by Mr Sebag Shaw and Mr Peter Rawlinson.

The first witness was Constable Philip Banyard, who had prepared a plan of the area where the shooting had taken place. He was followed by Detective Constable Thomas Macmaken, who had photographed the body of David Blakely in the mortuary.

The first major witness was Anthony Seaton Findlater. He detailed David Blakely's movements over that Easter weekend, and went on to admit that he had lied when Ruth telephoned and he had told her that David was not at the flat.

The next witness was Bertram Clive Gunnell, who had been with David in the *Magdala Tavern* and who had then witnessed the shooting outside. Gunnell had left the *Magdala* a few steps in front of David. As Gunnell waited at the passenger door, David, carrying a flagon of beer, walked around to the driver's side.

After the first shot had been fired, David began running around the back of the car. He was followed by Ruth and at one stage, she had told Gunnell to get out of the way. By now, David was on the pavement, running up the hill at the side of the *Magdala*, but Ruth pointed the gun and fired again. David Blakely fell face down on the pavement. Ruth stood over him and fired into his back.

Constable Alan Thompson, the officer who had been enjoying a quiet off-duty drink in the *Magdala*, then gave details of Ruth's arrest. Before the shooting, he had noticed a blonde haired woman looking into the bar, through the window. He thought nothing of it at the time, but later realised that it was the same woman who had fired the gun. Constable Thompson testified that, when he went outside, he saw Ruth standing with her back to the pillar between the two windows. She still had the revolver in her right hand.

Thompson was followed to the witness box by Ernest Pett, an ambulance driver, who had arrived at the scene at approximately 9.25 pm on 10 April. He noted the position of David Blakely's body, lying face down with his feet towards the public house and his head pointing up the hill. The body was placed inside the ambulance and Clive Gunnell accompanied it to the New End Hospital.

The next witness, Dr Elizabeth Beattie, was waiting for the ambulance at the hospital. She examined Blakely, at 9.45 pm and confirmed that he was dead. The body was still warm to the touch.

Doctor Beattie was followed to the witness box by Gladys Yule, who lived at 24 Parliament Hill. Gladys explained that she and her husband were walking down towards the *Magdala*, when they saw two men come out of the public house and stand near a car. A blonde haired lady, who she now knew to be Ruth Ellis, spoke to one of the men, and this was followed, almost immediately, by a flash and the sound of a shot. Further shots were fired and after the last one, Gladys felt a sudden searing pain in her right thumb. She realised that she had been hit by a ricochet and had to go to the hospital, by taxi, for treatment.

Doctor John Rea was on duty at the Hampstead General Hospital when Gladys Yule arrived at around 10.00 pm. He found a penetrating wound at the base of her right thumb, and a fracture of the first metacarpal bone. The bullet causing that wound had passed entirely through Mrs Yule's hand.

Further evidence of events at the hospital were given by Dr Albert Charles Hunt, who testified that he had examined David Blakely after he had been pronounced dead. Dr Hunt went on to detail the wounds in the body. There was an entry wound in the lower part of the back on the right hand side.

Tracing the path of this bullet, Dr Hunt finally found it in the tissues of the tongue. This bullet had caused wounds to the intestines, liver, left lung, aorta and windpipe.

The second injury was above the hip-bone on the left hand side, with an exit wound very close by. This bullet had merely penetrated through the fatty tissues. There were also other wounds on the inner left forearm and beneath the left shoulder blade.

Dr Hunt was followed to the stand by Ruth's other lover, Desmond Cussen. He began by admitting that he and Ruth had been lovers, albeit briefly, in June 1954, after the Le Mans race. He went on to say that on many occasions he had assisted Ruth in using make-up to cover bruises she had received from David, after a particularly furious argument. That brief exchange, was the limit of the questioning Cussen had to suffer and later developments might possibly suggest that other questions should have been asked.

Joan Ada Georgina Dayrell Winstanley, was the housekeeper at Egerton Gardens and she confirmed that Ruth and David had lived there together, using the surname Ellis. She was followed to the stand by three separate police witnesses.

The first of these was Detective Chief Inspector Leslie Davies, who gave details of Ruth's written statement, after she had been arrested and taken to Hampstead Police Station. This long statement included two important claims. The first was that, having decided on a course of action, Ruth had taken a revolver, which she had had in her possession for some three years. She said that she had obtained it from a customer at the club, in payment of a debt. The second claim was that she had then taken a taxi to Tanza Road

The second police witness was Detective Inspector Peter Gill, the officer who had actually written Ruth's words down, read them back to her and then got her to sign the statement as being accurate. The final police witness was Detective Constable George Claiden, who had been present at the post-mortem, carried out by Dr Hunt, on Easter Monday.

The final prosecution witness was Lewis Charles Nickolls, who gave evidence about the gun which was used to kill David Blakely. He had test fired the weapon and, comparing these bullets with those taken from the dead man, proved that the gun taken from Ruth Ellis was indeed the weapon which had caused Blakely's injuries. Nickolls was then asked if he might give an opinion, on the distance the weapon might have been fired from. Nickolls said that he had examined Blakely's clothing and found a bullet hole on the left shoulder at the back. The bullet used to cause this hole, and the corresponding wound on Blakley's body, had been fired from a distance of less than three inches. This was the only bullet hole which had powder burns associated with it. In Nickolls opinion, all the other bullets had been fired from a distance.

The defence did call Ruth Ellis herself. She made no attempt to deny culpability in any way. At one stage, Mr Humphreys, for the prosecution, asked Ruth, 'Mrs Ellis, when you fired that revolver at close range into the body of David Blakely, what did you intend to do?' Without emotion, Ruth replied, 'It was obvious that when I shot him, I intended to kill him.'

On the second day of the trial, the jury retired to consider its verdict at 11.52 am. After an absence of just fifteen minutes, they filed back to announce that they had found Ruth guilty of murder. She was then sentenced to death. The following day, her defence team announced that there would be no appeal. The execution date was set.

In the condemned cell at Holloway, Ruth Ellis, prisoner number 9656, wrote a number of letters. One of these, dated 12 July, was to David Blakely's mother. It began:

*Dear Mrs Cook,*

*No doubt these last few days have been a shock to you. Please try to believe me when I say how deeply sorry I am to have caused you this unpleasantness.*

*No doubt you will hear all kinds of stories regarding David and I. Please do forgive him for deceiving you. Has [sic] regarding myself, David and I have spent many happy times together.*

*Thursday, 7th April, David arrived home at 7.15pm. He gave me the latest photograph he had, a few days hence, had taken. He told me he had given you one Friday morning at ten o'clock he left and promised to return at eight o'clock, but never did. The two*

*people I blame for David's death, and my own, are the Findlaters.*
*No doubt you will not understand this, but perhaps, before I hang,*
*you will know what I mean. Please excuse my writing, but the pen*
*is shocking.*

*I implore you to try to forgive David for living with me, but we*
*were very much in love with one and other[sic]. Unfortunately,*
*David was not satisfied with one woman in his life.*

*I have forgiven David. I only wish I could have found it in my*
*heart to have forgiven him when he was alive.*

*Once again, I say I am very sorry to have caused you this*
*misery and heartache. I shall die loving your son and you should*
*feel content that his death has been repaid.*

The letter was signed, 'Goodbye. Ruth Ellis'

Questions still remained and Mr Victor Mishcon, Ruth's
solicitor, urged her to tell the truth, even at this late stage. No
taxi driver had been found who could remember driving the
distinctive blonde woman to Tanza Road, and Ruth's story of
having the gun for some three years, was also not accepted. On
the same day that Ruth wrote to David's mother, she also
wrote a letter to finally reveal the truth.

This letter was written the day before Ruth Ellis was due to
die. It was timed at 12.30 pm, by which time she had less than
twenty-four hours to live. It began:

*I, Ruth Ellis, have been advised by Mr Victor Mishcon to tell the*
*whole truth in regard to the circumstances leading up to the*
*killing of David Blakely. It is only with the greatest reluctance*
*that I have decided to tell how it was that I got the gun with*
*which I shot Blakely. I did not do so before because I felt that I*
*was needlessly getting someone into possible trouble.*

And continued:

*I had been drinking Pernod (I think that is how it is spelt), in*
*Desmond Cussen's flat and Desmond had been drinking too. This*
*was about 8.30 pm. We had been drinking for some time. I had*
*been telling Desmond about Blakely's treatment of me. I was in a*
*terribly depressed state.*

*All I remember is that Desmond gave me a loaded gun.*
*Desmond was jealous of Blakely as in fact, Blakely was of*
*Desmond. I would say that they hated each other.*

*I was in such a dazed state that I cannot remember what was*
*said. I rushed out as soon as he gave me the gun. He stayed in the*
*flat. I rushed back in after a second or two and said, 'Will you*
*drive me to Hampstead?' He did, and left me at the top of Tanza*
*Road.*

*I had never seen that gun before. The only gun I had ever seen*
*there was a small air pistol used as a game with a target.*

That same day, police officers tried to find Desmond Cussen,
to ask him about this confession. He was not at home and
would only be traced after events had come to their
conclusion. Ruth's statement was not, of course, made public
at the time, and for years afterwards, Cussen continued to
deny that he had given Ruth the murder weapon, or had taken
any part in the crime. Only now can the contents of Ruth's
final statement be revealed.

The following morning, Wednesday 13 July 1955, Ruth
Ellis, still only twenty-eight years old, was given a tot of brandy
to fortify her. She then walked calmly into the execution
chamber at Holloway prison, where she was hanged, by Albert
Pierrepoint. She was the last woman ever to be executed in the
United Kingdom.

# Appendix

**Female Executions in London, 1800–1955**

## *(1) Public Executions*

| | Location | Crime | Date |
|---|---|---|---|
| **1804** | | | |
| Ann Hurle | Newgate | Forgery | 8 February |
| Providence Hansard | Newgate | Forgery | 5 July |
| **1805** | | | |
| Mary Parnell | Newgate | Forgery | 13 November |
| **1806** | | | |
| Sarah Herring | Horsemonger Lane | Coining | 8 April |
| **1807** | | | |
| Elizabeth Godfrey | Newgate | Murder | 23 February |
| **1809** | | | |
| Mary Barrington | Newgate | Making a false oath | 22 February |
| **1810** | | | |
| Melinder Mapson | Newgate | Robbery | 13 June |
| **1812** | | | |
| Catherine Foster | Newgate | Making a false oath | 12 August |
| **1813** | | | |
| Sarah Fletcher | Horsemonger Lane | Murder | 5 April |

|  | **Location** | **Crime** | **Date** |
|---|---|---|---|
| **1815** | | | |
| Elizabeth Fenning | Newgate | Attempted Murder | 26 July |
| **1817** | | | |
| Sarah Perry | Newgate | Murder | 24 February |
| Elizabeth Fricker | Newgate | Burglary | 5 March |
| **1818** | | | |
| Mary Ann Jones | Newgate | Forgery | 17 February |
| Charlotte Newman | Newgate | Forgery | 17 February |
| Harriet Skelton | Newgate | Uttering | 24 April |
| **1820** | | | |
| Sarah Price | Newgate | Uttering | 5 December |
| **1821** | | | |
| Ann Norris | Newgate | Robbery | 27 November |
| **1826** | | | |
| Mary Cain | Newgate | Murder | 16 January |
| **1827** | | | |
| Amelia Roberts | Newgate | Robbery | 2 January |
| Mary Wittenback | Newgate | Murder | 17 September |
| **1828** | | | |
| Catherine Welch | Newgate | Murder | 14 April |
| **1829** | | | |
| Esther Hibner | Newgate | Murder | 13 April |
| Ann Mary Chapman | Newgate | Attempted Murder | 22 July |
| **1832** | | | |
| Elizabeth Ross | Newgate | Murder | 9 January |

| | Location | Crime | Date |
|---|---|---|---|

**1846**
Martha Browning    Newgate    Murder    5 January

**1848**
Harriet Parker    Newgate    Murder    21 February

**1849**
Maria Manning    Horsemonger    Murder    13 November
Lane

**1862**
Catherine Wilson    Newgate    Murder    20 October

## (2) Private Executions

**1870**
Margaret Walters    Horsemonger    Murder    11 October
Lane

**1874**
Frances Stewart    Newgate    Murder    29 June

**1879**
Kate Webster    Wandsworth    Murder    29 July

**1890**
Mary Wheeler    Newgate    Murder    23 December

**1896**
Amelia Dyer    Newgate    Murder    10 June

**1900**
Louisa Masset    Newgate    Murder    9 January
Ada Chard-Williams    Newgate    Murder    8 March

**1903**
Amelia Sach    Holloway    Murder    3 February
Annie Walters    Holloway    Murder    3 February

|  | **Location** | **Crime** | **Date** |
|---|---|---|---|
| **1923** | | | |
| Edith Thompson | Holloway | Murder | 9 January |
| **1954** | | | |
| Styllou Christofi | Holloway | Murder | 16 December |
| **1955** | | | |
| Ruth Ellis | Holloway | Murder | 13 July |

## Summary

| *Crime* | *Executions* |
|---|---|
| Murder | 24 |
| Forgery | 5 |
| Robbery | 3 |
| Attempted Murder | 2 |
| Making a false oath | 2 |
| Uttering | 2 |
| Burglary | 1 |
| Coining | 1 |
| Total | 40 |

# Source References from The National Archives

| | |
|---|---|
| DPP 2/4360 | Manning |
| DPP 4/2 | Manning |
| CRIM 1/6/1 | Manning |
| CRIM 12/9 | Manning |
| MEPO 3/54 | Manning |
| MEPO 3/123 | Bravo |
| HO 144/237/A52045 | Pearcey |
| CRIM 1/83/2 | Sach and Walters |
| CRIM 1/244 | Fahmy |
| CRIM 1/247 | Fahmy |
| DPP 1/74 | Fahmy |
| FO 141/796/10 | Fahmy |
| MEPO 3/1589 | Fahmy |
| CRIM 1/2492 | Christofi |
| DPP 2/2368 | Christofi |
| PCOM 9/1721 | Christofi |
| DPP 2/2430/1 | Ellis |
| DPP 2/2430/2 | Ellis |
| MEPO 2/9888 | Ellis |
| HO 291/235 | Ellis |
| HO 291/236 | Ellis |
| HO 291/237 | Ellis |
| HO 291/238 | Ellis |
| CRIM 1/2582 | Ellis |
| PCOM 9/2084 | Elllis |

# Index